THE LINES
THAT DIVIDE
AMERICA

THE LINES THAT DIVIDE AMERICA

RACE, PROTESTS, AND POLICE

JERRY WUCHTE

gatekeeper press

Published by Gatekeeper Press
3971 Hoover Rd. Suite 77
Columbus, OH 43123-2839
Copyright © 2015 by Jerry Wuchte

Layout Design by: Mr. Merwin D. Loquias

ISBN: 9781619849181
eISBN: 9781619849198

Printed in the United States of America

Dedication

This book is dedicated to Alexis Samuels (Boyd). I met this six year old angel in May of 1989, a year before I became a police officer. Occasionally when talking about my law enforcement career I've been asked what was the worst call I ever ran.

I've never hesitated for a second recalling while working at University Hospital Ambulance Service my partner and I being dispatched to a GSW (gunshot wound).

We arrived before law enforcement and were waived into the scene by bystanders. On the porch was a man writhing in pain from three gunshot wounds trying to ignore his pain and telling us to check on his daughter. My partner started treatment on the man as I entered the house and saw blood on the floor and then the partially clothed body of a young girl I later found out was Alexis.

She was on top of the telephone and I imagined whatever had happened she must have been trying to call for help. I could see small puncture wounds on her little body and wasn't sure if she was alive.

I turned her over slowly and she surprised me with wide open eyes accompanied by shallow rapid breaths. I'll never forget her change of expressions. Alexis looked terrified as I turned her over and saw her face, I spoke calmly to her holding her hand and reassuring her she would be okay. Her face relaxed as she looked at me with my uniform.

I called to my partner for something to try to apply pressure to what I noticed were at least three stab wounds. A nearby steak knife seemed about the size of the weapon that may have caused these injuries. My partner had the medic bag vigorously treating the father while a backup ambulance and law enforcement were arriving.

I knew I needed to apply a trauma dressing before moving her and hated to leave her side but made eye contact as I told her I would be right back. In the seconds it took to sprint and grab the dressing and return, Alexis had closed her eyes and she would never open them again. I grabbed her and ran her to the ambulance while a police officer helped my partner load the father into the ambulance.

With a scene time of only a couple of minutes we were speeding to the hospital. Law enforcement from several agencies blocked every intersection and escorted us for the almost ten mile trip to the trauma center. When we arrived nurses and doctors were standing outside the emergency room door ready to fight to save the lives of this father and daughter.

Alexis had suffered a double pneumothorax due to her injuries and her little chest filled with air causing her lungs to collapse on the ride to the hospital. CPR had been initiated by an EMT who had rode in with my partner from the scene, but less than an hour after arriving at the hospital pronounced Alexis dead. Her father would fight for several days and surgeries before he succumbed to his injuries.

I would later find out the father had died believing his little girl was still alive after doctors were scared if he knew he may give up his will to live. The father had his daughter for weekend visitation and the murderer had done some yard work and arrived demanding payment. Allegedly the work was not completed which led to the father refusing to pay until it was completed.

At the trial I saw a beautiful picture that Alexis had been taken for school and remembered a local newspaper story of her classmates a few weeks after the murder graduating and leaving her seat open.

It's a hard thing knowing you were the last person this child would ever see. It has always been my hope that the horror she experienced before we met in that couple of minutes that we knew each other was somehow alleviated. I like to believe that it gave her some level of peace by seeing a uniform, feeling a comforting touch, and hearing a calm voice that cared about her.

I never forgot her and a little more than a year later I would leave the ambulance service and start a twenty year career in law enforcement. There are many other children, women, and men I will also never forget, but the memory of that fragile precious girl reminded me often why law enforcement exists and should be supported.

Contents

Introduction *13*

Chapter 1 *The Blue Line: Law Enforcement in
America* *19*

Chapter 2 *Street Gangs: America's Deadliest
Terrorists* *67*

Chapter 3 *America's Classroom: Defiant,
Disinterested, and Angry* *79*

Chapter 4 *Racism: Real, Perceived, and
Manufactured* *111*

Chapter 5 *Violence and Hate in Entertainment* *143*

Chapter 6 *The Millennials: Disconnected and
Discontent* *163*

Chapter 7 *The Politics of a Divided Nation* *181*

Conclusion *191*

Introduction

Television screens fill with images of crowds protesting the police. Teenagers assault officers in broad daylight by throwing rocks and bricks. As night falls, businesses are burned and looted. Instead of shock and outrage, marches against the police commence and spread to major cities across the country. Reporters and commentators seem to sympathize with the protesters as though the police have brought this on themselves. Protesters block streets calling for dead cops, and those calls are answered as unsuspecting officers are murdered around the country.

Many Americans are left in a state of disbelief when one story after another features white police officers killing black men. Video clips and eyewitness accounts provide jaw dropping evidence that seems irrefutable that black men are under attack. For some it is so outrageous to comprehend police officers targeting African Americans that they dismiss the allegations. Others see each story as a confirmation as what they have been taught, told, and experienced about being black in America.

Analysts speak as though the civil rights movement has reemerged and speculate on the causes from institutional racism to poverty. If you look closely you'll see that it is not Dr. King and the SCLC burning those buildings in Baltimore and Ferguson, and the officers they are protesting against are not the KKK with their hoods off.

From 1990 until 2010 I worked law enforcement in Augusta, Georgia. My career included time as a field training officer, SWAT team member, narcotics detective, school resource officer, and road supervisor. For the next five years I was a public school teacher and coach. In this book, I explain how my background, education, and experience has given me a unique insight on race in America and how it relates to law enforcement and education.

Before entering law enforcement I bounced around a number of jobs that gave me an opportunity to work with and meet people of different races, religions, and socioeconomic standing. I ran a drill press in the machine shop at the local EZ-GO factory, building golf carts. I bagged groceries, washed dishes, cooked fast food, worked in a convenience store, and did lawn and building maintenance, which included cutting grass, mopping floors, and cleaning bathrooms.

My public service career started in 1988 at the Burke County Emergency Management Agency, where I cross-trained as an EMT and firefighter. I loved EMS and worked for several ambulance services and also in the geriatric ward of the state mental health facility. I'm very proud of my time in law enforcement, which had its share of challenges and rewards.

After several attempts to go to school while working full-time, in 2008 I finally obtained my associate's degree from Georgia Military College. I transferred to the local university and two years later earned my bachelor's degree, then left law enforcement to begin teaching. Over the next few years I added a master's degree while teaching high school history.

As a teacher I hold certifications in economics, political science, and U.S. and world history with a gifted endorsement. I've also completed a number of training classes as a volunteer with the American Red Cross. I have long respected public service workers and have always looked for opportunities to serve. In my own life I feel very blessed and hope when I'm done I have lived a life with purpose and service to others.

As a parent I have four kids, including my oldest son from my first marriage. I've been married to my current wife for over twenty years, and like many parents we have dedicated ourselves to raising our children. I started volunteer coaching in 1995, first my kids teams and then high school and middle school.

I grew up in a family that stressed hard work over education. My two oldest sisters dropped out of high school but worked very hard, both getting their GEDs and continuing their education. My youngest sister went to technical school and works as a medical assistant. My father worked in a factory for over forty years, and my mother worked retail in different department stores. My mother grew up working in the groves in Florida with her parents, never realizing they were poor.

I contemplated writing this book for over a decade, and each year as new incidents in our country came up I felt guilty for not taking the time to put this together sooner.

Every author dreams of writing a book that will change the world, and a few like Thomas Paine's *Common Sense* and Rachel Carson's *Silent Spring* actually have. I can only hope that I express what seems obvious: that as Americans we realize how truly blessed we are and how united we should be. My biggest fear is that we live in a society that is so splintered into different groups and so partisan that we are losing sight of how great our country is and failing to enjoy what we have.

The title *The Lines that Divide America* refers to how we are separated, labeled, and taught who and what we should love and hate. The discussion will focus on race relations as they relate to law enforcement, gangs, education, sports, and entertainment.

As you progress through the book I encourage you to be brave and open your mind. I'm not asking anyone to change political views or other beliefs. I do ask that you consider opinions based on your own experiences and not just what you have been taught and told. All too often we take opinions from teachers, celebrities, and so-called news outlets and make them our own, even though we have no personal reason to do so.

Chapter 1

The Blue Line:
Law Enforcement in America

The Thin Blue Line is a common symbol and phrase used to describe law enforcement. Some officers consider it the line they guard between order and chaos. Others see it as a brotherhood and a way for officers to stand together. Some officers reject the blue line ideology altogether and see it as an opposition to community-based law enforcement.

I worry about what the history books will say about police officers in the 21st century. It is almost universally accepted that law enforcement unfairly stops, searches, detains, arrests, imprisons, and kills African Americans. Even conservative commentators have conceded this point, and the U.S. Justice Department has released findings that law enforcement often discriminates and violates the civil rights of minorities. Some would say that if the U.S. Justice Department said it, it must be true. Even people who distrust the government will readily accept this allegation because it fits their existing belief; those same people will continue to criticize the government at every other opportunity when they don't agree.

For law enforcement it is an absurdity and incomprehensible that anyone would believe that in America, in the 21st century, they could or would target African Americans or any other race. Not every African American or civilian believes they do, and not every white person or even officer believes they don't.

So who exactly are these police officers who are being accused on a daily basis of stopping, detaining, arresting, and killing citizens because they're black? Police officers working today grew up in the 1970s, '80s, and '90s, not in the divided nation that existed in the 1950s and '60s. They grew up in the same diverse and accepting American society as their critics. They idolized African American athletes like Michael Jordan, Walter Payton, and Tiger Woods. They paid to see movies starring African American celebrities like Denzel Washington, Samuel L. Jackson, Morgan Freeman, and James Earl Jones, and the list could go on and on.

The vast majority of officers working the streets of America over the last twenty-five years do not possess the racist views that existed in many parts of this country generations ago.

Today's officers do not understand how anyone can conceive of the idea that they would dare stop or suspect anyone of committing a crime based on their race. The *Denver Post* reported the results of a 2014 survey that 95 percent of the 724 officers who responded to the study feel that police officers deal fairly with members of the minority community. The sample size was small but I believe this would be the sentiment of how most law enforcement officers feel across the country. Officers I've spoken with make extra efforts to ensure they are courteous and fair when dealing with African Americans, well aware of the scrutiny each of these encounters are under.

While officers feel like they interact fairly with all citizens, an August 2014 report, *Gallup Review: Black and White Attitudes Toward Police* by Frank Newport on gallup.com, showed their attitudes are not shared by the communities they serve. The report demonstrated double-digit differences in attitudes of black respondents compared to white respondents on how ethical law enforcement officers are and about racism being a factor in incarceration rates. It reveals what we probably knew that regardless of the opinions of white Americans and law enforcement, African Americans believe there is a problem.

It's as though critics of law enforcement believe that when an officer puts on a uniform he or she becomes a racist. It seems every day there is a new story about how racist cops and politicians are quick to weigh in on both sides. Even the president on several occasions has confirmed racial bias in the criminal justice system, adding to the legitimacy of the stories. President Obama in November 2015 asked the media to maintain perspective on the way they report about terrorism, warning that they may empower these groups, but those sentiments and press requests seldom apply when dealing with race or law enforcement.

Law enforcement officers are the same people that you interact with every day and are as diverse as America itself. Instead of being in the KKK or a bunch of white supremacists, officers are the people you work out with at the gym and the people you cheer with at the sports bar. They are Republicans, Democrats, and independents. Police officers are Christians, Muslims, atheists, straight, and gay.

Protesters love to say they don't oppose all police officers, but a great deal of the signs carried, the chants, the social media posts, and campaigns are against all law enforcement. The message often advocates and has shown to result in violence against officers, although admittedly not every protest is meant to be anti-law enforcement or advocating violence.

Criminals take advantage of protests or any other gathering, including celebrations, as an opportunity to cause havoc. People of good will also join in, feeling as though this is a movement they want to be a part of, buying into the allegations that racist cops are roaming the streets looking to arrest and kill African Americans. It can be even more upsetting to officers when respected high-profile Americans join the protests. Protesting and hating cops has unfortunately become fashionable.

Law enforcement officers have always been open and easy targets. They patrol our neighborhoods in bright, noticeable cars while wearing distinguishable uniforms. These marked uniforms and cars are not to fight a war but instead so they are recognizable to the citizens who need them. This high visibility is intended to deter criminal activity and reassure citizens that the police are looking out for them.

Police officers, especially in major cities, spend a large part of their shift answering calls assisting low-income citizens who may also be minorities. During this time they will not grow to hate the citizens they serve but instead feel compassion and build relationships—not necessarily friendships, but the types of relationships that are only known by selfless individuals who serve others. Think of your nurse or doctor. An officer could develop anger and frustration at the criminals who victimize the citizens they have grown to care about.

Officers do not choose which laws they want to enforce or which areas will have a larger police presence. In our data-driven society, the human element is often taken out of decisions regarding where to deploy resources. Crime rates, not individual opinions, dictate which areas have more officers assigned to them.

Increasing the police presence in neighborhoods with a goal of reducing crime can have an unintended consequence. It can result in a higher probability of police and citizen encounters, with an escalation of minor incidents such as traffic stops. This happens as more officers are in the neighborhoods and may feel compelled to be active.

If a department commits resources to an area, they expect those resources to yield statistics in the form of stops and arrests. The pressure to produce results does not only come from supervisors but more importantly the citizens. A neighborhood with a high crime rate also means it has a large number of victims. Those victims look to officers for protection and to rid their neighborhood of criminals, and that goal is what drives every stop and every encounter.

It doesn't mean the officer always gets it right or always does it the right way, and in those instances officers realize they will be held accountable. Officers are extensively trained that each decision they make can have criminal and civil repercussions.

Not every predominantly African American neighborhood has a high crime rate or the increased police presence that a high crime rate demands. In Augusta,

Georgia, as in other communities, there is no shortage of affluent and middle-class African American families. The members of these families are no more likely to see or encounter law enforcement than their white neighbors.

The public wants law enforcement to curtail crime rates, and to do that officers must be aggressive. Law enforcement officers are tasked each day to protect victims and apprehend offenders. A good police officer is both curious and suspicious, but what exactly leads to police suspicion or stops can vary from officer to officer. It should not be surprising that the things like clothing choices, tattoos, facial hair, and piercings will draw attention from a police officer but will also draw attention from anyone else, which is often the intention of why we dress, look, or act a certain way.

Ironically, officers themselves possess some of the same characteristics that draw second looks from police officers. These characteristics are not race specific and would apply if you were white, black, Hispanic, or Asian. While these things will get you looked at, they should not result in a police encounter, an encounter that always carries the possibility of the suspect being stopped, detained, arrested, or—if the officer feels threatened—killed.

The one thing that will lead to a police encounter is committing a crime. This could be any crime, and often the person committing the crime believes their violation is so minor in nature that it does not justify being stopped. Someone with an expired tag or not wearing a seatbelt may think the police should have stopped someone speeding or running red lights. People speeding and running red lights think the police should go after drunk drivers. Drunk drivers think the police should get the drug dealers, and drug dealers think the police should get the murderers.

People think of officers as actually being the law, but they are only the enforcement part of the law. Elected legislators make those laws, and the officers working the street do not choose which laws they want to enforce. Officers engage criminals because that is their job. A failure of an officer to act when faced with a minor violator is the equivalent of a cashier refusing to check you out if you have a small order. When people go to work, they are expected to do their jobs. People who don't do their jobs don't keep those jobs, and law enforcement officers are no different.

Drug couriers, serial killers, and terrorists know exactly how to avoid getting a second look from law enforcement. Avoiding suspicion helps criminals go unnoticed for long periods of time. Looking suspicious has nothing to do with race but more to do with appearance and behavior.

While trying to look like a tough guy on the weekends, I'll often alter my own appearance. To do so I'll skip the daily shave, throw on a pair of worn jeans, and put on a sleeveless shirt to show off my tattoo.

It should be no surprise that anything done to look cool, trendy, or tough will draw more attention. That attention could be positive or negative, but regardless of why you chose a look or behavior, it will not only get a closer look from friends but also from law enforcement.

Things like wearing a hoodie, hat, scarf, or anything obscuring your head or face is of course perfectly legal, but it looks more suspicious and draws more attention when you have these things on. The hoodie of course become infamous after Trayvon Martin was killed, but the hoodie was seen as a threatening image long before Trayvon. Millions of Americans in the 1990s saw widely circulated drawings of Ted Kaczynski, known then as the Unabomber and the hoodie appeared to be a way for him to obscure his identity.

Long hair on a guy is also more suspicious than having short hair; the longer the hair, the more suspicious. Again, not illegal but it still makes you stand out. Tattoos have become increasingly common, and many officers love them as well, but having a tattoo makes you more suspicious than not having a tattoo, and the more tattoos, the more suspicious you appear. Facial hair: If you have a beard, you are more suspicious than someone who does not have a beard. The longer the beard, the more suspicious you look, and again the more you stand out.

Of course, you can have tattoos and a long beard and wear a hoodie over your skull cap and still be a law-abiding, upstanding citizen—many people are. These things alone should not lead to a police encounter that could result in being stopped, arrested, or—if the officer feels threatened—killed. If you choose this look, it is probably because you want to stand out, express yourself, or be, like me, an old guy trying to look tough or cool.

Appearance and dress in today's society is carefully planned. One of the biggest hobbies is the "selfie," taking a picture of yourself and posting it on social media. The decision to wear sloppy, saggy, oversized pants and T-shirts with big statements is not casual but instead a concentrated effort to portray a certain image. Expressing yourself and individuality has become the norm.

The notion of law enforcement harassing people because they are black gained a renewed popularity during the 1980s and '90s. As murders of young black men involved in drug-and gang-related crimes soared, officers stepped up efforts to combat drug trafficking in the inner cities. Catchy terms to thwart drug interdiction efforts took hold. Terms like "racial profiling" and "driving while black" came about as drug dealers and their lawyers sought technicalities to have searches and convictions overturned. Police officers even wanting to stop and search people and cars has always been motivated by the desire to get rid of or at least curb drugs and reduce the violence related to them, and the only people they want to harass are criminals.

Stopping and searching a car, stopping and searching a person, or even searching a house is one of the most dangerous things an officer can do. Officers don't do these things for fun. It's never fun. It is an attempt to stop crime and save the lives that are lost due to criminal behavior. The behavior of the criminal along with the officer's experience and training can influence if these incidents go bad.

Most of us would not challenge or taunt a trained MMA fighter, a boxer, or an armed soldier. If someone chooses to provoke one of these individuals, they would expect an unfavorable outcome. Officers are routinely taunted even when not on a call.

Like all of us, when an officer panics their "fight or flight" reaction kicks in. For an officer, that reaction must be to fight. People should realize that when dealing with an officer, even an officer who appears calm, that that officer is trained to react instantly to danger, with deadly force if necessary to eliminate that threat.

Most officers will never use deadly force. What they will do is throughout each shift on almost every call prepare in their mind to draw and use their weapon. A person walking toward an officer with their hands in their pockets will get an officer's attention as a potential threat. As surveillance cameras, cellphone videos, dash cameras, and body cameras become standard, the officers' actions and the evaluation of the suspect will be broken down frame by frame.

Officers are trained extensively to confront and react to violent situations. They spend more and more time each year preparing for active shooters and terrorist attacks.

The training involves eliminating the threat. When training to use deadly force, officers are placed in calm, relaxed positions with guns holstered facing targets. The targets on the range turn quickly and as the threat arrives and they must react instantly to eliminate the threat. The targets will turn for a few seconds and then turn away, forcing the officer to draw and fire without evaluating each time what they are shooting. The target is always a threat but this quick-reaction training can have deadly consequences if the perceived threat turns out not to be an actual threat. Classical conditioning, or a Pavlovian response, programs an automatic reaction to certain triggers. It's like when your alarm goes off in a dark room and you instinctively hit the snooze button. When an officer gets into a panic situation, they will often reach for and draw their firearm even if the threat is unknown.

If an officer makes the decision to use their weapon, their training and firearm proficiency often will result in the death of the suspect they are engaged with. The drawback is that what triggers the officer's panic and response could be an unarmed suspect who is fighting or fleeing. While that action may generate panic and a response, it may not reach the imminent threat level required for using deadly force.

Law enforcement officers are trained if they are involved in a fight that they cannot lose. If they lose, the criminal goes free, and if someone is a danger to an armed trained police officer, then they are an even greater danger to the public. It would be an easier day at work for an officer to just look the other way, avoid confrontations, and allow criminals to flee. This, however, is not what we expect or need from our officers.

In my public service career, I've held children while they have taken their last breath. I've held the hand of grown men as they've succumbed and died from gunshot wounds. I've pulled men off the women they have beaten unconscious. I've given CPR and first aid to victims ranging from infants to the elderly.

As a teacher I've worked with students for hours after the school day has ended, on Saturdays, and even through the summer to help them pass required tests for graduation. My combination of careers may be unique, but the things I've done and seen in those jobs are not. Many officers, EMS workers, and teachers have seen and dealt with much worse. I know, however, that if I put back on a police uniform tomorrow, I would be hated and not trusted by many of the same people whom I interact with on a daily basis.

As an officer, thankfully I never had to shoot or kill anyone, but I have been in a few situations in which it would have been justified. As an officer, I was threatened, spat on, slapped, punched, and kicked, and the only gunfight I was ever in I lost. As I lay in the hospital bed recovering from those gunshot wounds, a week before my second son was born, I never once wished I had killed the man who had tried to kill me. I again do not feel like that is unique, and believe that officers involved in shootings sincerely wish there had been an alternative.

I truly believe that today's law enforcement officers are yesterday's Vietnam veterans. Like the Vietnam vets, I think we'll look back on how we treated these public servants and owe them an abundance of apologies. These veterans and today's police officers were both given unpopular jobs by politicians. Both have been protested by citizens who will never know of the sacrifice and service that these men and women have provided for the very people who've protested them.

The catchy anti-police slogans of our time, including "Hands Up, Don't Shoot," "I Can't Breathe," and "Black Lives Matter," are direct attacks on the officers who would put their own life at risk without hesitation for any one of the protesters. Most Americans don't think of law enforcement officers as warriors and protectors. They are instead seen as an inconvenience. Law enforcement means being stopped and given a ticket when you're running late for work. Law enforcement breaks up the party at which you're having a good time. It's only when we are victims or in danger do we appreciate them.

Criminals benefit from the public hate and distrust for law enforcement. It allows them to victimize communities and even portray themselves as victims when confronted by police officers.

The purpose of law enforcement is, through education and enforcement, to achieve voluntary compliance of the laws. If you want to put police officers out of work, help them lower crime rates. A department with a low crime rate is unlikely to get additional funding for more officers. Recognize that an officer patrolling your neighborhood is not looking for his next victim, but is there to protect you and your family from harm. Reject the criminal propaganda and slogans and report crimes and criminals. Officers don't deserve your protest; they deserve your gratitude.

Men and women who enter law enforcement do so to serve others, but that's not to say they always do the right thing. Every department that makes arrests sooner or later is going to have an officer use excessive or unjustified force. These incidents will usually be triggered by fear or anger, not racism. Occasionally officers may see warning signs in a coworker and not know what to do. They may notice behavior that could lead them to suspect an officer is frustrated or depressed.

Officers must look for and be willing to confront another officer's behavior head on and before it escalates. I've seen officers fired for misconduct, and coworkers typically said that they were not surprised. It is disturbing that coworkers would notice something and just let a fellow officer go down rather than intervene at the risk of offending or betraying them. Law enforcement is a job with little direct supervision, and to be successful you must create a culture of accountability.

As a narcotics detective, I asked citizens to reject the criminal's plea not to support and cooperate with law enforcement. I see no difference in an officer covering for another officer than I do for criminals covering for other criminals.

I was lucky as a young officer to be assigned to a partner who never cared if he fit in. He was committed to catching criminals but never cut corners. He often said if he couldn't catch them (criminals) the right way, then he wouldn't catch them at all. He vowed to never put me in a position in which I might feel the need to lie or cover up, and in over fifteen years of working together he never did.

Another person who reinforced the need to be honest was then-Magistrate Court Judge Carl Brown. Most of the cases city officers made went before Judge Brown, who had a reputation of giving the officers the benefit of the doubt, which I know to some doesn't make him sound like a great jurist. I was warned right away that if Judge Brown ever caught an officer in a lie or misled him, they would never win another case in his court.

In addition to honesty, which I think most officers possess, what I think helped me through a twenty-year career was not taking the challenges of the job personally. I learned that people who hate the police didn't hate me; in fact, they didn't even know me.

My partner also never got angry at criminals for trying to get away. This unique quality was important, because in some of the cases where officers use unjustified and excessive force, it involves a fleeing or resisting suspect. I'll never forget one of my lieutenants drawing and pointing his gun at a man running from a stolen car following a pursuit. Remarkably, it had only been about ten years earlier that shooting a fleeing felon would have been legal.

Vehicle pursuit policies often require abandoning chases for minor offenses when the offender enters a heavily populated area. Once in these areas, the danger of accidents with injuries and fatalities are increased so chases are broken off.

This is not the case when arresting individuals. Most departments have policies that involve using what is called the minimum amount of force necessary to affect the arrest. The offense the suspect is being arrested for is not taken into consideration. There are such things as felony vehicle stops and executing high-risk arrest warrants that may allow for officers to plan the encounter, but most arrests are spontaneous and involve one officer and one suspect. This one-on-one will lead to a murderer and a shoplifter getting the same treatment, and the level of force used will depend on the level of resistance by the offender.

It may seem as though law enforcement should enact a policy of not using force when making arrests for minor or nonviolent offenses. The problem is that law enforcement would then see almost all minor offenders refuse and resist arrest. Once criminals determined which offenses did not justify forcible arrests, those crimes would skyrocket.

What departments can do is empower officers to make the call. That may involve sometimes letting a criminal go just as they do when they break off a vehicle pursuit. As with vehicle pursuits, if the offender is identified or known to the officer, then the idea of arresting them at a later time, hopefully without incident, is more likely. Also similar to charging a driver with fleeing, an additional charge of resisting should be added so the incentive to resist is eliminated. There will still be discrepancies on when and how much force should be used, and some people will never accept officers using any level of force.

When officers use excessive force it usually comes down to failing to control anger. Nothing will excuse an officer who loses control, but it's hard to comprehend the amount of verbal abuse and threats an officer endures.

The ride to the jail is the greatest opportunity for prisoners to berate the arresting officer. I actually stopped wearing my wedding band because it became common to hear from the backseat what was going to be done to my wife. I still had prisoners asking if I had a wife or girlfriend, and when I said no the threats would often shift to my mother.

The older patrol cars actually had cages, and on several occasions I have been spat on while driving. Most prisoners will act calm and normal until they get a good chance to spit in the officer's face. Most people would say if someone spit in their face they would react violently, but for an officer that would not be justified. You instead learn how to position yourself to keep prisoners facing away, but it's still a fairly common occurrence.

From comments to spit, officers are constantly forced to use restraint and recognize that a lot of these actions are attempts to provoke them. Most officers recognize when they have gone over the line. They also realize what the consequences of excessive force are, including the termination of their job and career.

A more complicated reason officers use force is because they are scared and in fear for their life. This is complicated because it's impossible to know what is in someone's head. Law enforcement has no more justification to use deadly force than the average citizen. It's just that the job increases the likelihood of placing officers in more of these situations than an average citizen.

All officers will experience some level of fear during a career, and at times that fear is justified. Where officers can go wrong is if they panic. Some officers are blessed with nerves of steel; they quickly evaluate situations and make good decisions. Officers with military training and experience may be more prepared to cope with stressful situations.

Departments can and do incorporate training scenarios that help officers learn to function and make good decisions in high-stress situations. A bigger challenge is identifying an officer who does not respond well in high-stress situations and then determining what to do with them.

If an officer makes it through the extensive hiring process and training, it's not easy to get rid of them just because supervisors and coworkers think that person is not up to the job. In some areas police unions and representatives will vigorously defend members with little consideration or knowledge of the officer's value or liability to their department.

Another concern we see is that following protests, officers become less aggressive. Officers can slip into a bunker mentality as they ban together and forget that anyone in the community supports them. The blue line can then become a dividing line between the officers and the public. It's easy to fall into an "us versus them" mentality, and that defeats the whole purpose of law enforcement.

Officers must remember that in a free and democratic society, if it is truly "us versus them," then "them" wins. Terms like the "War on Drugs" have officers going to work with an expectation of confrontation and conflict. Officers and departments must rethink how they approach and interact with citizens. They must make themselves a part of the community, and not be perceived as an invading force attempting to conquer.

One tactic I taught new officers was from the movie *Roadhouse*. Patrick Swayze's character told the bouncers to be nice, be nice, and be nice, until it was time not to be nice. I noticed that I was in a lot of fights when I was a younger officer and much fewer as I got older. I realized it was often how I spoke to people and that I was expecting a confrontation and often got it.

As I got older, I also noticed I had less hostility with suspects following the arrest even at times when I did use force. The suspect would remember "the nice" I had demonstrated and not feel like I had just arrived looking to arrest them. It's hard to imagine treating every encounter with kindness and sensitivity, but that's just what has to be done.

Every officer at one time or another will encounter an off-duty officer or maybe one of their family members or friends and have to make a decision about whether to write a ticket or make an arrest. They also have to decide if they can do someone a favor and try to look out for them. If that person has committed a serious crime, it shouldn't matter who they are; they should be arrested.

If it's the chief's or sheriff's buddy, they'll be treated with more consideration and respect knowing they have a law enforcement connection. In cases of minor offenses, they may be more likely to get a break or a warning.

Departments should train officers to treat each citizen, including criminals, as though they are an off-duty officer or a fellow officer's family member. It's a simple question an officer can ask himself or herself: "Is this how I would treat an off-duty officer or an officer's family member if I had to arrest them?"

Following the Ferguson riots, claims were made that too many white officers were working African American neighborhoods. It's disgraceful to say that white officers can't police African American neighborhoods. It reminded me of a teacher who said openly that predominantly

African American schools like Laney where I taught should only hire African American teachers.

We should appreciate anyone who is willing to step up and sacrifice. If we judge where an officer can work based on their race and then ask officers to treat all races they encounter equally, it seems a little hypocritical.

If an officer is unable to go into a neighborhood and feel a connection to the citizens they are protecting, then that and not the officer's race should be taken into consideration. A problem that can exist is if an officer feels superior to the people living in the area they work. If an officer feels that way, it can be just as big of a problem as racism.

An officer can make good decisions and act appropriately thousands of times; it only takes a single incident or a momentary lapse in judgment to end a career. Anger and fear can sometimes be allies, but they must be recognized and the officer must always remain in control. Officers must expect to be provoked and challenged and never give in to the provocation.

The media angle of hostility between law enforcement and the African American community cannot be underscored. Historical images of law enforcement officers attacking civil rights protesters with dogs and firehoses appear daily in textbooks and on posters, on television, and in movies.

From cartoons to comic books, newscasters, politicians, comedians, actors, musicians, and athletes all reinforce the stereotype that law enforcement officers are racist and out to get "the black man." With overwhelming images portraying officers as incompetent, crooked, and racist, the challenge of serving the public has never been greater. A big reason people do not like police officers is because they are required to enforce unpopular laws.

Legislators may need to consider decriminalizing some types of behavior that forces officers to make arrests. Lawmakers must understand that if you create a criminal law it will at some point require an arrest. This tasks officers to make those arrests with whatever force—which could escalate to deadly force—needed to complete the arrest.

It would be up to local and state governments to decide which laws would meet this criteria, but all nonviolent offenses ranging from illegal gambling and not paying child support to marijuana possession must be considered and decided if incarceration of the offender increases public safety.

I think of some popular cases such as Wesley Snipes going to jail for tax evasion or Martha Stewart for insider trading. Of course, offenders need to be punished, but we should consider the idea that prison be reserved for those who pose a danger to society.

During my daughter's junior year of high school, a parent of a girl she played softball with was arrested for a sexual assault on another young female softball player. The man struck a plea and instead of jail time became a registered sexual offender and attended every softball game that season. I think of all the cells filled with people who are not dangerous while this predator never spent any time in jail past being booked.

Another case that comes to mind of someone who needed to be in jail but was somehow allowed on the streets was following a night my partner and I had stumbled upon several men standing around a vacant alley. One of the men was found with a loaded handgun, and a check showed he was a convicted felon. About a month after arresting this man, he murdered a pawn shop owner while stealing more guns. Officers need to be allowed to focus on dangerous individuals such as this man and know that when they are caught they will be held.

Officers' actions are constantly critiqued, and they should not be forced to arrest the same felons over and over. When officers do make arrests, they are influenced by stress, fear, and anger. These factors may sometimes explain an officer's excessive use of force, though as stated earlier it never excuses it. Consider a 3 a.m. 911 call followed by a hang-up with no answer when the dispatcher calls back. It could be kids playing on the phone or it could be a family being held hostage. An officer walking up to that door must be prepared for the worst, but if the officer approaches the door with a drawn weapon and it turns out to be children, it could end up on the news and end his career.

We live in a world where the danger of mass shootings and terrorist attacks are very real possibilities. We need our law enforcement officers well trained, well-armed, and ready to act. They need to be focused on threats that most of us don't want to think about instead of being worried about being ambushed by someone wanting to make a political statement.

Many people are so certain law enforcement officers target African Americans that they will not even listen to reason or statistics about the real dangers to us all. One thing missing for critics of law enforcement is the smoking gun. We don't see the clear evidence that confirms all of this suspicion once and for all. Certainly in today's age of social media, secret recordings, emails, and text messages, someone would have come forward.

It would seem to reason that by now a law enforcement officer would have stepped up in a moment of conscious and admit they went after people just because they were black. If it's law enforcement as a whole, there must be a memo or policy out there confirming this institutional racism within departments.

We don't and won't see this confession or documentation because law enforcement officer's agree: black lives and all lives matter, and that's why they are out there 24/7. Not only is there no police opposition to "black lives matter," this movement has no opposition at all. I have not heard or read of one person saying black lives don't matter.

Concern by officers that pulling over African American drivers for minor offenses, such as not wearing a seatbelt, will be perceived as racial profiling can make officers reluctant to make these stops. The consequence of this reluctance can have deadly results.

In 2006, a U.S. Department of Transportation report, "Race and Ethnicity in Fatal Motor Vehicle Traffic Crashes 1999–2004," showed a higher number of traffic fatalities among African American children compared to other groups, with a low percentage of seatbelt usage listed as a factor.

Officers have a right to be concerned. A 2011 report by the U.S. Department of Transportation, "Determining the Relationship of Primary Seat Belt Laws to Minority

Ticketing," implied that pulling over and citing minority drivers for seatbelt violations may in fact be a form of racial profiling. If drug dealers and their high-priced lawyers hadn't manufactured the "driving while black" defense to being stopped, it's reasonable to believe that some of these children may still be alive.

We've also seen increased crime and murder rates in areas in which protests have taken place. A November 14, 2015 article by Ian Simpson at reuters.com, "Baltimore homicides top 300 for year, worst since 1999," asserts that the rise in crime coincided with that year's riots. The article cites a criminologist at the University of Baltimore as blaming drugs, guns, and gangs while the FBI director acknowledged police were holding back in fear of being accused of brutality. Officers want to protect and serve, but many may feel that their presence and service is not welcome. When criminals including drug dealers and gang members can get the police to back off, their victims suffer.

If you still believe police officers ride around trying to find black men to confront and kill, take a few more things into consideration. Officers like other people go to work looking for a smooth shift and a safe return home. It doesn't stand to reason that an officer would go out and make his workload heavier and shift busier by initiating and escalating incidents with anyone, not to mention with African Americans when the officer is fully aware of the potential and likelihood of accusations of racism.

But the criminals, by making these accusations, may be able to engage in more criminal activity, get outstanding charges dismissed on technicalities, create doubt in trials, and even benefit from lucrative cash settlements if officers and departments can't prove the encounter wasn't based on race.

Let your common sense guide your opinion of law enforcement. Is an officer who goes into a job with low pay and dangerous working conditions with the principle of protecting and serving really out there because he is a racist and wants to find an excuse to harm African Americans? It is much more likely that drug dealers and gang members who embrace mottos like "Thug Life," "Get Rich or Die Trying," and "F the Police" are motivated to turn communities against law enforcement.

Criminals do not want people to cooperate with the police, and they use threats and violence against those who do. Gang members' claim officers come into low-income neighborhoods and mistreat people who live there, yet anyone caught talking to the police or trying to build a positive relationship is labeled a "snitch," and they are in danger.

The economics of law enforcement is also something people should consider before jumping on the anti-police bandwagon. Neighborhoods with high crime rates are often low-income areas. The willingness of municipalities to dedicate resources to combat crime should be welcomed with gratitude and support instead of protests and scorn.

The only people who benefit from anti-police rhetoric and protests are criminals. Every protester is not a criminal, but every protester against the police has bought into the lie that we have large numbers of racist police officers roaming the streets of America.

In a CNN.com article by Jennifer Agiesta, "Race and Reality in America: Five key findings," cites an October 2015 poll that 64 percent of Americans believe racial tensions in the last ten years have increased. Gangs and the entertainment industry have tried to turn gang culture into black culture. I wish I was surprised by this poll, but each day our country seems more divided.

If historically there was such a thing as black culture, instead of just American culture, it would be distinguished by faith and family. Gang members consider the gang their family and demand loyalty; betrayal against the gang is punished with beatings and executions. Even if a gang member rapes, robs, and murders, fellow gang members are expected to support them. When criminals can convince the public that the police are the bad guys, what the public is unintentionally doing is supporting the people who murder and sell drugs to the children of this country.

We'll never know how many men and women who would have made wonderful, compassionate officers decided to go into another profession after watching anti-police protests. We'll never know how many of our best officers have left the job because of these protests. Even worse, we also have no way of knowing how many officers will see that suspicious person or car and instead of following their instincts will go the other way and avoid a potential confrontation, which is exactly what the criminals want out of this so-called movement.

If you are African American and get stopped by the police and you think it was because you are black, it was not. I can remember pulling a minivan over one night for running a red light. Prior to the stop I could not see the race or sex of the driver. The driver turned out to be an African American man with his wife and children. He quickly disputed that the light had turned red before he made it to the intersection.

Both the man and I were courteous during our conversation and as I issued the citation he asked about his chances of "fighting" the ticket. I let him know of his court date and encouraged him to appear if he felt like he did not commit the offense. His next line was "who are they going to believe, me or you?" I paused for a second and replied that they, either a jury or the judge, would try to figure out what my motivation could be for stopping him if he had not run the light.

The idea that African Americans are stopped because of their race is said so often, people of all races believe that it must be true. There is no need to make up violations; it is not as if there aren't thousands of people out committing them each day. There is also a great chance, as with the stop I recalled, that the officer could not even identify your sex or race prior to pulling your car over.

The other accepted myth is that African Americans are followed around stores. If you are African American and you think the clerk in the store is following you around because you are black, they are not. There is a good chance the person working there is a millennial and they would be more likely to join an anti-police protest than profile a customer based on race. If the loss-prevention officer even wanted to watch you, they would watch with the store cameras from a security room instead of following you around.

As much as we would like security and law enforcement to be proactive, they are and always will be reactive. Crime rates in certain neighborhoods are not higher because more police are present; more police are present because the neighborhood already has a higher crime rate.

Problems for police officers can exist when deadly force is used even if it is deemed justified. The most detrimental thing that the public can hear is about overkill. In November 2015 a Chicago police officer was arrested for murder after shooting a young man a reported sixteen times. While the man was armed with a knife, the video that was released showed him struck and go down while the shots continued.

We can't know what was going on in the officer's head, but shooting a suspect sixteen times sounds like a fully loaded magazine of fifteen with one in the chamber and every round being fired until the gun ran dry. That amount of rounds fired seems to indicate rage. What led to this possible rage in this specific incident we may never know, but suspects being killed with multiple hits is not unique.

An alternative to rage that can lead to multiple rounds being fired is what law enforcement calls sympathetic shooting. It can be the difference between a suspect being shot once, twice, or even twenty times. It can lead to a suspect being shot by one officer or by five. In a sympathetic shooting an officer makes the decision to fire their weapon and other officers on the scene respond as well, even though they may not have identified the threat personally.

Law enforcement training does not allow for shooting to wound or firing warning shots. If an officer determines a threat and makes the decision to use deadly force, they are trained to fire two shots to the chest, often called a "double tap." If the target remains, a single shot to the head is taken followed by evaluating the threat.

Once the decision to use deadly force has been made, the officer will fire until the threat is eliminated. Some may remember in 1999 when four NYPD officers fired forty-one shots in killing a man named Amadou Diallo. In 2013 a Texas officer was terminated after firing forty-one shots himself at a suspect he killed. Whether it's sympathetic shooting, rage, or fear, these instances of overkill are difficult to explain and understand.

With over 900,000 officers on the streets each day across America, officer involved shootings, especially where suspects are shot this number of times are extremely rare. When it does happen it is so widely publicized that it is difficult to ever forget. The public perception of officers firing two shots instead of forty is very different. Officers are trained to use the minimal amount of force necessary to make an arrest, but I've never heard the term "minimal amount of deadly force." It may seem like dead is dead, but the perception of the incident will live on. Training should remind officers that every round, every trigger squeeze should have its own justification.

The same week the Chicago officer was arrested for murder, sparking massive protests and the removal of the superintendent of the police department, another man was arrested for murdering the nine-year-old son of a rival gang member. Both killings were terrible, and in each one a mother lost a son. The gang retaliation shooting reminded us that law enforcement officers are needed to fight evil and every officer must make the effort to portray themselves to the public as the protectors that they are.

The year 2015 saw its share of officer-involved shootings and protests, but it also saw law enforcement officers risking and sometimes losing their lives. Mass shootings in Colorado and California saw officers engage suspects who had already taken lives and undoubtedly save others.

I wish every officer was respectable and every shooting was justified, but this book would have no credibility if I pretended they were. It is crucial that officers who are burned out and others who never should have been hired must be identified and removed before they are allowed to tarnish the badge. Recognizing these officers is the responsibility of both the departments and fellow officers.

Departments should have an anonymous procedure for frequent peer evaluations of officers' attitudes and behavior. Departments are more than capable of forming their own questionnaires, but if asked I believe many officers would identify coworkers they do not feel comfortable working with. The brotherhood of law enforcement should be a brotherhood of righteousness, and when an officer ceases to behave in a righteous way they no longer deserve to be in the brotherhood.

The evaluation process can't stop with fellow officers; it needs to extend to everyone officers interact with, including suspects. I know that last one is a rough concept, but getting feedback about the arrest and interaction that followed is crucial. It could be done at booking, hours later, or even days later, but it's important that each suspect get a chance to respond. While you may have some of the suspects looking at the feedback as a chance to pay back to the officer for arresting them, it's a misconception that every arrest is confrontational. If trends are noticed for one officer and not others making similar arrest, that could indicate a need for intervention.

The other feedback should be questionnaires from the complainants and victims. These should generally be favorable toward the officers as they are the people they are helping. Combined, which is the only way they should be looked at, these types of feedback can give a pretty good picture of who we have working our streets. Officers will also be aware that they are being evaluated by everyone they come in contact with, and that alone will encourage them to maintain positive and professional interaction.

Getting rid of a fellow officer may seem distasteful and fly in the face of the brotherhood code, but it must be done. Think of all the good officers as clocks that help things run orderly. Think of a bad officer as a time bomb. The time bomb may look a lot like a clock, and the clocks may even think the time bomb is a clock like they are, but it's not.

The time bomb doesn't help keep order; instead it creates disorder. Once the time bomb goes off, if the clocks are too close they'll be destroyed along with the time bomb. The only hope is that they recognize the time bomb and get rid of it before it goes off, and no one should feel guilty about that.

Chapter 2

Street Gangs:
America's Deadliest Terrorists

Islamic terrorist groups such as Al-Qaeda and ISIS pose enormous threats to the U.S. and the world. Their gruesome acts grab headlines and spark international outrage. History has shown that we cannot ignore these external threats, and the world looks to the United States to combat these terrorist organizations. However, when it comes to killing United States citizens, these global terrorists kill only a fraction of the men, women, and children murdered by American street gangs.

Rightfully so, we teach American students that the KKK is a white terrorist organization, one that has killed an estimated three thousand to five thousand African Americans in its hundred-plus-year history. As disturbing as those numbers should be to all of us, in the last ten years, according to the FBI Uniform Crime Reports, more than seventy thousand African Americans have been murdered. The overwhelming majority of these men have been killed in drug and gang-related violence by other black males.

These gangs, which date back to the 1960s, have taken more American lives than any single war in over a hundred years. Many of these gangs originated in the Los Angeles area, and the most visible of these is also one of the deadliest, the Crips. They are responsible for the murders of tens of thousands of African American men, yet the entertainment industry has brushed aside these domestic terrorists and embraced gang members as hip-hop artists and actors, enabling their gang mentality to spread across the youth of this nation while collecting millions of dollars and awards along the way.

Instead of being shunned by society, celebrities with acknowledged gang affiliations like Snoop Dog and Ice Cube are portrayed as lovable family characters. I don't want to use too much of this section on the Crips alone because other gangs are equally destructive and murderous. The Crips are, however, the most popular of these gangs.

The Crips are responsible for wiping out generations of young African American families, and by promoting what they call "their reality" they have encouraged millions of people to emulate their dress, speech, and criminal behavior. In addition to murder and drug dealing, street gangs—in what they proudly call "pimping"—engage in sex trafficking of young girls and women.

American street gangs have distributed drugs worth billions of dollars on the streets of America, and while doing it perfected something called the drive-by. If you're not familiar with the drive-by, it is when cowards get in a car and drive through a rival gang's neighborhood, shoot guns at kids, and then speed away before the opposing gang can respond. It's equally acceptable for gangs to just drive by and shoot up houses or apartments and let bullets strike whomever may be on the other side of the wall.

Thousands of children and elderly citizens with no gang affiliations have been killed over the years in these drive-by shootings, yet gangs and gang members continue to grow in acceptance and popularity. As a middle and high school teacher, I've seen kids of all races and ages emulating the gangs, and as a nation we aren't even appalled by it.

Some may disagree with the categorization of the Crips and other gangs as being terrorists, but if they are not then we need a title worse than terrorist. The fascination with criminals is nothing new; they have been glamorized for generations. The difference in gangs today and outlaws of the Old West or the Prohibition era gangsters is that modern street gangs are less organized and are especially dangerous as they try to prove themselves. Gang members routinely commit crimes against helpless, unsuspecting victims as initiations or just to pass time.

Domestic gangs threaten and take more American lives than all of the illegal immigrants (at least the ones who aren't in gangs) and Islamic terrorists. This includes any gang you can think of; there are no good guys in gangs. Hell's Angels, Aryan Brotherhood, Latin Kings, Crips, Bloods, MS13, Italian mobs, Russian mobs.... You name the gang and they are responsible and should be equally despised for spreading drugs, death, and destruction across America.

The existence and tolerance of these gangs draws a dangerous line between a hardworking productive society and lawlessness. Americans have always known gangs existed in the major cities, but were slow to acknowledge that they had spread across the rest of the country.

Initially when it came to gangs, many cities were in denial. This was largely because the street gangs at that time did not meet what the definition of a gang was then. Gangs were then expected to have organizational standards including rank and power structures. What made us not identify them as gangs is exactly what made them so dangerous: no accountability and a randomness to their violence that continues today.

The next level was the glamorization and embracing of gangs in America. This was done through movies, television, and music, with some of the current and former gang members I discussed earlier becoming celebrities. Today small groups of teenagers simply ban together and start gangs, often naming the gang after a street or a neighborhood. Pick a neighborhood or a city and simply put "boyz" or "posse" behind it and you've probably named a local gang. These startup gangs use the entertainment industry—including movies, music, and television—as a blueprint for ruthless criminal activities and behavior.

Successful movies such as *Scarface* and *New Jack City* are commonly referenced in hip-hop and rap, and drug dealers I've arrested have expressed open admiration for the characters in these movies. Today's generation is more connected and has even more exposure than in the past.

The 2015 blockbuster movie *Straight Outta Compton* glorified gang life and portrayed law enforcement as crooked and racist. This movie was presented as a true story, and many people who saw it will accept it as fact and attempt to pattern their life after the characters, many of whom went on to great success.

Gangs have managed to redefine what acceptable behavior in our society is. While you don't have to be a gang member to use obscene language in public or wear your pants low enough to see your underwear, these things are influenced by gangs.

Most Americans may not realize that by taking gang behavior lightly, it condones their behavior and existence. One ESPN commentator, who I'm sure is not a gang member, signs off routinely with a "deuce" sign, once again from the Crips street gang. It has for some reason become a compliment to tell someone that they look like a gangster—or telling them that something they have done is gangster. We don't think of that as saying you look like a murderer and a drug dealer. Instead of accurately portraying gang members as the people who kill and poison our children with drugs, they are often worshipped.

In addition to gang behavior in mediums discussed, children and adults can become a virtual gang member in video games. We sell video games in which kids can commit every level of criminal activity imaginable. It's not even like kids are sneaking around and looking up games online; parents openly buy them and are rarely aware of the disturbing content.

Gang influence can be found in almost every aspect of American society, including dictating what is acceptable and what is not. When I grew up in the 1980s, when a person white or black said the "n" word, the whole room would gasp. Gangs have made this vulgar term more common than at any time in history.

If massacring this country's young men each year isn't enough, if distributing drugs across the nation doesn't disgust you, then think about how gangs have promoted the treatment of our daughters, wives, mothers, and sisters. I don't remember before the emergence of gang popularity people routinely referring to women as "bitches" and "whores" (usually pronounced "hoes"). I guess it's less offensive for some reason to say "ho" than "whore." It is so common that even females refer to themselves and other women with these terms, and it's often not said or taken as an insult.

In a 2011 National Gang Threat Assessment report on fbi.gov, there were an estimated 1.4 million gang members responsible for up to 90 percent of violent crimes in some neighborhoods. The 2013 National Gang Report (NGR) cites numerous studies that gang participation is rapidly increasing. Additionally in a 2010 Office of Juvenile Justice and Delinquency Prevention study, 45 percent of high school students and 35 percent of middle school students acknowledged that gangs are in their schools.

Every year I worked law enforcement and every year I've taught I've seen behavior associated with gangs grow. Seeing gang signs thrown and colors worn were once cause for discipline or police intervention. Today students write gang-related symbols on their arms and notebooks, and parents would think it ridiculous if we contacted them about it because they often don't see a problem with it.

If we want to erase the lines in our country and come together, we have to recognize the things and people that divide and destroy us. Gangs and people who embrace, emulate, and defend them are at the top of the list. This country has gone through several periods where it looked as though we were destroying ourselves and managed to turn it around. That turnaround is coming, hopefully sooner rather than later, and when it does it will be because we reject the type of behavior that street gangs promote.

If my contempt for gangs and drug dealers seems in contrast to much of America's acceptance, it's because I've seen what they really stand for. I've seen the bodies gangs leave on the street. I've seen the addicts stealing from their families so they can buy drugs from the gangs. I've known of young girls prostituted and passed around gangs as though they were property. I've known young men beaten and raped by gang members in jail. So to all of the gang members turned celebrity, I've seen up close what you really represent. I can only imagine the things officers in major cities with even larger gang populations try to put out of their head when they go to sleep at night.

Chapter 3

America's Classroom:
Defiant, Disinterested, and Angry

It was an unlikely progression of life that I would ever meet Dr. Tonia Mason. I had spent the previous twenty years chasing criminals while Dr. Mason had worked her way up as a classroom teacher to become the principal of the high school she had graduated from.

In my last month of college I sent emails to a dozen local high schools, and Dr. Mason was the first to reply. It was her first year as a principal and she was looking for new teachers with new ideas.

My first teaching job would be in one of the neighborhoods I spent patrolling for most of my career. Laney High School was named after Lucy C. Laney, who founded the school after the Civil War to provide an education to African American children in Augusta, Georgia.

After being labeled as one of the lowest performing schools in the state and nation, Laney was designated as a turnaround school. This gave Laney a multimillion-dollar school improvement grant that partially went to teacher bonuses for reaching benchmarks with student improvement. The grant also equipped the school with the latest classroom technology while bringing in experts from around the state to provide the staff with the latest teaching strategies.

Additional money was allocated to rebuild the school, which was in such disrepair that many people I explained it to refused to believe it. The school was infested with rats, which teachers sometimes captured with boxes and baskets. The roof leaked, and following heavy rain classes were routinely relocated while the custodians removed puddles of water.

What the school did have was a brand new football stadium, considered one of the nicest in the state, especially for a school of that size. Laney also had a brand new, beautiful basketball gym, which was the pride of the school as they competed in boys and girls basketball state championships almost every year.

While Laney was known as a basketball and football powerhouse with highly regarded coaches and players, finding a staff willing and able to teach in a challenging school atmosphere was more difficult.

In the three years I worked with Dr. Mason I grew to admire many things about her, and she treated me with respect and support during the time I worked with her. She was a private person, but after being diagnosed with cancer she continued to lead the school with a dignity and strength I'll never forget.

I don't want to make this my life story, but by sharing some of the things about Laney, I'm sure I will shed light on what goes on in many schools across the country. Despite her own success, Dr. Mason openly expressed that she believed African Americans were still discriminated against in jobs, education, and society in general. Even with these beliefs, she without hesitation hired a white male former police officer. Instead of thinking I would be the worst person for the job, she thought I would be the best.

While working at Laney, I was one of the few white teachers—and for some students the first white teacher they ever had. The student population was more than 99 percent African American and economically one of the lowest in the state.

My experience as an officer was a benefit when stressful situations occurred, and I felt a genuine connection with the students knowing the challenges many of them returned to daily in their neighborhoods.

I was able to build great relationships with the students. I soon found myself teaching afterschool programs, Saturday school, and remediation classes in the summer for students who had failed the Georgia High School Graduation Test. I also helped coach the girls' softball team and started a peer tutoring club and a history club.

The school had many brilliant, kindhearted students who would be near the top of their class at any school in the country. The biggest reason Laney was an underachieving school was that students did not show up to class. I know it's going to seem unrealistic, but on a typical day a class of thirty students would have ten or more students absent. Some students accumulated forty or more absences throughout the year and remained enrolled. This is not saying Laney is a typical school for absences, but I do believe there are many other schools with this problems.

Because Laney had one of the highest dropout rates in the state, the staff was reluctant to withdraw students. Instead of withdrawing students who refused to attend, grade recovery programs were implemented to try to help raise the graduation numbers.

While trying to keep kids enrolled, it was easy to see that many students did not want to be in school and parents did not want to send them. It was only under the threat of criminal prosecution that parents were forced to send their reluctant students.

Many students would openly admit attending school for the extracurricular activities and would do just enough classwork to be eligible to participate. The band, football team, and basketball team had reputations of excellence, and most students wanted to be a part of one these squads.

Teachers felt the pressure not to take away the reason some of the kids were still enrolled, so a minimum effort was rewarded with at least a passing grade. It was not unusual for a coach, principal, counselor, or parents to check on a star athlete to make sure they remained eligible to play or accept a scholarship.

If the athletes were failing a class, teachers would be asked if they could figure out what needed to be done to "recover" their grade. Athletic scholarships put additional pressure on teachers since it meant that failing a student could take away the opportunity for college—and in the student's mind, a pathway to becoming a professional athlete.

As an athlete at Laney you could expect to be honored and awarded throughout the year. The school had its share of solid student athletes, but they were rarely the ones interviewed after a big game or getting the full-ride scholarship.

The face of Laney was not the kids who came to school each day keeping up with their classwork. It was not the student who could tune out distractions and made the honor roll for four straight years. If these kids were lucky, they would figure out a way to put a few small scholarships together, take out a student loan, and maybe get into a community college.

If the school thought they were doing the athletes a favor by lowering the standards, they were frequently reminded. In the short time I was at the school, several athletes from previous years would return home from college after one semester because they had been unable to handle the academics.

Growing up in the South, I was raised to be a football fan. We'd often gather with friends and families to watch or attend Georgia Bulldogs and Atlanta Falcons games. Laney changed my perception of what goes into creating the top-tier athletes we cheer for each week. In school, the elite athlete is allowed to behave with a disregard for the academic and behavioral requirements other students are held to.

Because of their attitudes, many teaches disliked the athletes and some said they found it difficult to cheer for the athletes knowing what poor students they were. I had my share of confrontations, but it made me think about how we are all responsible for this. To be honest, my decision to be a teacher was initially because I wanted to get paid to coach. Volunteer coaching and working with athletes had been something I had always enjoyed, and my own kids had gotten so much from sports.

Teaching gave me a chance to see the message we send to students, and the message is clear: athletes are superior to students. Students know that academic excellence will never be celebrated or rewarded at the level of athletics.

Laney, as with other schools, strived to have each student graduate and go to college or technical school. In talking to students, many of them believed being a professional athlete was in their future. All too often it seemed like the kids with dreams of being the next NBA, WNBA, or NFL stars were low-performing students. Some of these students holding onto this dream lacked the talent to even make the school team. Sadly they would also be the least likely to have a backup plan and would be offended if you tried to tell them it wasn't going to happen.

Teachers would try to stress that even if a dream of sports stardom is realized, an education is still important. That message does not resonate with students who see their low-achieving classmates get a full ride to a major college.

Students see sports as the "ticket" to fame and fortune, and in today's America they are right. Students are inundated with dozens of channels dedicated to sports, and hundreds of games and events are broadcast each week.

Sports like football and basketball that generate revenue will try to find loopholes around academic standards to get athletes into their schools and onto the field or court. Many of these athletes playing collegiate sports would not be accepted to the schools if held to the same academic standards as the general student body.

From the educational aspect, little can be done with college sports in their current state. One of the things that can be done to help rescue the educational system in America is to focus on building good students and citizens and not just great athletes.

The most radical thing we can do that would have an immediate consequence is to eliminate any scholarship or compensation given to athletes that is not equally available to the general student body of a school. Ivy League schools, which are among the top educational institutions in the world, do not give athletic scholarships. These elite schools also limit practice and game schedules so that they don't conflict with academics.

The elimination of athletic scholarships would force students with sports aspirations to focus on academics to obtain scholarships, and then play sports. College athletics make an enormous amount of money, but that does not create lower tuition for other students; on the contrary, tuition goes up while college coaches can now become multimillionaires.

In addition to paying coaches large salaries, they also spend considerable amounts of money flying teams around the country. The U.S. government and taxpayers provide funding to many of these schools that manage these large sports programs. Students even take out loans to pay tuition and fees, including athletic fees, to cover these costs. If the federal and state government wanted to flex their muscle on these schools, they could limit or withhold funds on a school that can "afford" to pay a coach $6 million a year.

With the massive amount of money spent on education and after-school programs, many of which include character education, we need to think about the schools' role in the progression of racism in America. The interaction between children of all races in pre-K and kindergarten can be heartwarming and give us hope for tomorrow. These children haven't been contaminated with the stereotypes or told who they should and should not like at that age. Very few five-and six-year-olds are angry, but over the years we'll make sure they are.

As they grow older some kids decide they don't like school and are angry simply because they are forced to attend. Other kids seem constantly angry, and I've often wondered why so many young people are angry.

When I left law enforcement to teach at an inner-city high school, I was treated with an acceptance and respect that I rarely experienced as a law enforcement officer.

Even after telling the students I had been an officer, many would say they hated the police, yet they never treated me any differently. The students also interacted with the school's public safety officer in a friendly, respectful manner.

The hardest part of being a police officer was that I dealt with people on the worst days of their lives. I looked forward to teaching and getting to know people on a different level. I knew the influence teachers had on my own life. I thought of my favorite high school teacher, Mr. Solomon Jones, a former police officer turned history teacher—just as I was twenty-five years later.

I never thought about Mr. Jones being African American until he taught us about the civil rights movement. I soon realized that I didn't grow up or live in the same world as Mr. Jones did. I didn't understand how he was teaching about historical events in the present tense. It was 1984. Vanessa Williams was Miss America, many of the country's favorite entertainers and athletes were black, and the school I was attending was almost a perfect split between the races. The lesson he was teaching about racial strife existing in present-day America was news to me.

I found the conversation having what I'm sure was an unintended consequence. Instead of thinking about racial equality, I started thinking of things in terms of black and white like I had never done before. It was not about white being better than black or even about white guilt. Instead, I felt irritated. I was irritated that I was being lumped into a history of racist behavior, and I could feel division taking hold in the classroom along racial lines as the lesson was being presented.

By advocating that the struggle continues, Mr. Jones almost ensured that it would. If Mr. Jones was saying that the fight for my black classmates continued, then I realized the struggle had to be against something and someone. That something was racism, and that someone was white people, a category that I fell under.

The message seemed to be that if my friends and classmates were going to fight racism, they would see me as the enemy and would then be fighting against me. I didn't feel like I was fighting against them and I certainly wasn't for racism. This would be the first time I felt as if I were being attacked, but far from the last.

I remember my response to Mr. Jones, who encouraged debate. My heart was racing as I wondered what his reaction might be or what my comment might provoke. I'm not sure of my exact wording, but my question was about having groups and organizations designed to help only African Americans. To black Americans this sounds ridiculous and racist, probably because these organizations grew in response to the Jim Crow era following the 1896 U.S. Supreme Court *Plessy v. Ferguson* ruling. This case led to decades of "separate but equal" laws being enacted in many places across America. Many parts of the country were successful at the *separate* but rarely at the *equal*, which is why we must avoid separating our society based on race today.

Mr. Jones had grown up in the shadow of the Jim Crow era. Even though school segregation had been overturned unanimously by an all-white Supreme Court in 1954, America still remained divided in the years following the decision. While pockets of resistance to equality remained, the Civil Rights Act of 1964 and Voting Rights Act of 1965 further showed the rapid dissolving of racial lines in America.

Recently, for the first time, we seem to be moving away from equality and into an era in which everyone is angry. We see white Americans angry because they feel attacked, just as I did in Mr. Jones' class. I've heard the question about how a group formed to help only white Americans would be perceived.

Except for white supremacists who are outcasts in our society, no rational white American expects or wants anything in the new millennium to be "whites only," and they don't relate to or sympathize with whites who benefited during the Jim Crow era. Because of this, anything designated or named "black," from an organization promoting education to a television network, can be seen as a double standard.

Many of these groups including the more militant ones such as the Black Panthers have also provided social services in areas that they were desperately needed. The concern for our country is when groups no longer seek equality and instead exist and promote separation.

Most of my students lived in neighborhoods and went to predominantly African American churches. Even while having little interaction with white people, almost every student felt as though white people discriminated against them. If this wasn't from their own experience, then it could only be from what they were taught and told.

I can address firsthand what students are taught. Teaching standards and curriculum dictate exactly what—and in many school districts, how-information is taught. With the implementation of Common Core, the methods of teaching are increasingly controlled.

Georgia, for example, has twenty-five standards for teaching a year of United States history. Nineteen of the twenty-five standards contain information about racism, oppression, and discrimination. By the time I finish teaching each year, I can understand why students hate the police and the white man.

When First Lady Michelle Obama's highly publicized and often misinterpreted comments about being "proud to be an American for the first time" caused a firestorm—with some agreeing with her and others criticizing her—it should not have been a surprise. After all, she and most of us went to school in America. While the history of our country is not all positive, we teach a lot of the negative aspects of America and little about her greatness.

Georgia is considered conservative, so it would be hard to imagine that the rest of the country is not teaching a similar curriculum. Some of my colleagues and friends who don't teach history doubt the idea that nineteen of twenty-five history standards we teach relate directly to race. To help the students retain the information, lessons incorporate video clips and pictures to help the kids visualize the history they are being taught.

Below I've listed the Georgia Performance Standards, which are available at georgiastandards.org. The first letters are for Georgia Performance Standards, the next two letters are for social studies, and the next three are for U.S. history and then numbered. The letter given is the element. See for yourself the standards and think of how this barrage of information shapes the minds of our children.

GPS SSUSH1 The student will describe European settlement in North America during the 17th century.

a. Explain Virginia's development...and the development of slavery.

GPS SSUSH2 The student will trace the ways that the economy and society of British North America developed.

b. Describe the Middle Passage (the part of the Triangle Trade Route that brought African slaves to the Americas), growth of the African population.

GPS SSUSH5 The student will explain specific events and key ideas that brought about the adoption and implementation of the United States Constitution.

c. Explain the key features of the Constitution... and the issue of slavery.

GPS SSUSH6 The student will analyze the impact of territorial expansion and population growth and the impact of this growth in the early decades of the new nation.

a. Explain the Northwest Ordinance's importance...on slavery.

GPS SSUSH7 Students will explain the process of economic growth, its regional and national impact in the first half of the 19th century, and the different response to it.

b. Describe reform movements, specifically temperance, abolitionism (movements and resistance to those movements to end slavery), and public school.

GPS SSUSH8 The student will explain the relationship between growing north-south divisions and westward expansion.

a. Explain how slavery became a significant issue in American politics; include the slave rebellion of Nat Turner and the rise of abolitionism.

b. Explain the Missouri Compromise and the issue of slavery in western states and territories.

e. Explain how the Compromise of 1850 arose out of territorial expansion. (This standard would also cover the Fugitive Slave Act.)

GPS SSUSH9 The students will identify key events, issues, and individuals relating to the causes, course, and consequences of the Civil War.

a. Explain the Kansas-Nebraska Act, the failure of popular sovereignty, Dred Scott case, and John Brown's Raid.

GPS SSUSH10 The student will identify legal, political, and social dimensions of Reconstruction.

b. Explain efforts to redistribute land in the South among the former slaves and provide advanced education (Morehouse College) and describe the role of the Freedmen's Bureau.

c. Describe the significance of 13th, 14th, and 15th amendments.

d. Explain Black Codes, the Ku Klux Klan, and other forms of resistance to racial equality during Reconstruction.

GPS SSUSH13 The student will identify major efforts to reform American society and politics in the Progressive Era.

    c. Describe the rise of Jim Crow, Plessy v. Ferguson, and the emergence of the NAACP. Describe the impact of the railroads in the development of the West; include the transcontinental railroad, and the use of Chinese labor.

GPS SSUSH14 The student will explain America's evolving relationship with the world at the turn of the twentieth century.

    a. Explain the Chinese Exclusion Act of 1882 and anti-Asian immigration sentiment on the west coast.

GPS SSUSH15 The student will analyze the origins and impact of U.S. involvements in World War I.

b. Explain the domestic impact of World War I, as reflected by the origins of the Great Migration.

GPS SSUSH16 The student will identify key developments in the aftermath of WWI.

d. Describe modern forms of cultural expression; include Louis Armstrong and the origins of jazz, Langston Hughes and the Harlem Renaissance.

GPS SSUSH19 The student will identify the origins, major developments, and the domestic impact of World War II, especially the growth of the federal government.

a. Explain A. Phillip Randolph's proposed March on Washington, D.C., and President Franklin D. Roosevelt's response.

GPS SSUSH21 The student will explain the impact of technological development and economic growth on the United States, 1945-1975.

b. Describe the impact television has had on American culture...and news coverage of the Civil Rights Movement.

GPS SSUSH22 The student will identify dimensions of the Civil Rights Movement, 1945-1970.

a. Explain the importance of President Truman's order to integrate the U.S. military and the federal government.

b. Identify Jackie Robinson and the integration of baseball.

c. Explain Brown v. Board of Education and efforts to resist the decision.

d. Describe the significance of Martin Luther King, Jr.'s Letter from a Birmingham Jail and his I Have a Dream Speech.

e. Describe the cause and consequences of the Civil Rights Act of 1964 and the Voting Rights Act of 1965.

GPS SSUSH23 The student will describe and assess the impact of political developments between 1945 and 1970.

b. Describe the political impact of the assassination of President John F. Kennedy; include the impact on civil rights legislation.

d. Describe the social and political turmoil of 1968; include the assassination of Martin Luther King, Jr.

GPS SSUSH24 The student will analyze the impact of social change movements and organizations of the 1960s.

a. Compare and contrast the Student Non-Violent Coordinating Committee (SNCC) and the Southern Christian Leadership Conference (SCLC) tactics; include sit-ins, freedom rides, and changing composition.

GPS SSUSH25 The student will describe changes in national politics since 1968.

b. Explain the impact of Supreme Court decisions on ideas about civil liberties and civil rights; include such decisions as Roe v. Wade

(1973) and the Bakke decision on affirmative rights.

As you can see, it is a yearlong process of how evil and oppressive the white man has been. Black students completely buy into and relate with the history of hardship for African Americans and feel pain and anger as though this was their own experience.

U.S. history is not the only time students are exposed to how bad the white man has been, and how much of a victim African Americans are. These lessons are introduced in elementary school and infused into other subjects.

At Laney I saw students given assignments to write about issues such as modern-day slavery. As students' research and write, they often become angry. The African American students are constantly told the white man hates them and discriminates against them, and this creates in many students a defiance.

Black history is taught so well that almost every student at Laney could tell you about Frederick Douglass and Harriet Tubman, but many students did not know or remember anything about Paul Revere, FDR, or John F. Kennedy. Black History Month adds extra emphasis on the struggles African Americans have endured, and at no time is black history seen as a celebration.

I teach history because I believe we learn from our mistakes. I encourage tolerance and would never want to teach a revised history or ignore the past of America. The truth for African Americans and the rest of us is that we are fortunate to live here. Most immigrants whose ancestors probably arrived after the ancestors of most African Americans were poor and faced discrimination and difficulties of their own. We teach very little of these immigrant groups in U.S. history. A few things that are mentioned is the arrival of different groups at Ellis Island and the development of social services to help care for many of them.

Students don't feel lucky or blessed to be a part of this nation because they are so overwhelmed with how terrible we are and have been. Schools alone are not the only reason for pessimism. It is also not exclusive to one race or political party. The news headlines are filled with death and destruction, violent video games are the most popular, and the top movies in ticket sales are action packed with plenty of death scenes and explosions.

Many people who think they are struggling in modern-day America may still own a car and likely have cable television, air conditioning, and name-brand clothes, and even a lot of our poor and homeless have cell phones.

We teach history so vividly that even powerful and privileged African Americans claim to be victims of racism. President Obama grew up in the tropical paradise of Hawaii, attended two Ivy League universities, is a best-selling author, has become a multimillionaire, and was elected as a U.S. senator and a two-term U.S. president, and when he is criticized supporters feel as though he is a victim of racism.

It seems ridiculous to many Americans that people who are successful still believe and propagate the idea that all African Americans are the victims of racism. This brings me back to Laney and some of the things that students were told by administrators and school officials that reinforced or created their anger.

For example, in a speech telling the students how proud he was of them and how well they were doing, the school superintendent told a gym full of students and parents that it was important to highlight their talents because everyone thinks of students at Laney as criminals.

Dr. Mason, in what was also meant to be a motivational speech following the Trayvon Martin killing and George Zimmerman acquittal, called the male students to the auditorium. While telling the students how important education was, she also stated they could now be legally killed walking down the street just because they're black.

It seemed outrageous to hear kids told these things, but these messages come from highly educated, successful people in positions of authority, so why would a student question them? The saddest part is that Dr. Mason and the superintendent at that time, Dr. Roberson, truly believed what they told the students.

Telling students that by being African American they are hated and discriminated against not only makes them angry but also hopeless. Many students may ignore the opportunities in front of them and, due to what they've been told, feel like they should not even try.

In the classroom a hopeless student feels no reason to try, no reason to respect, and worse, no reason to live. Hopeless students do not look forward to the future, so they have no motivation to succeed. I've had students in my class refuse to do anything, even refuse to put their name on a piece of paper.

The phrase told to too many kids by too many people is that by being black they will likely wind up "dead or in jail." I've heard children told this hundreds of times, both in person and on television programs. Someone at some point must have thought this was motivational, but again it creates hopelessness and anger. It's no surprise that many kids growing up hearing this hate the police, teachers, and other forms of authority.

It's easy to say these are bad kids, but they are reflective of what they are taught and told. Once we decide to unite this country instead of asking kids to fight a fight that no longer exists—once we start trying to raise good citizens and stop trying to raise athletes, entertainers, and kids who live by the get-rich-or-die-trying philosophy—we will do better.

Chapter 4

Racism:
Real, Perceived, and Manufactured

While teaching and studying history, we often try to determine what preceded and even caused certain events and changes in America. It's never one thing that led to things like the Revolutionary War, Civil War, or Civil Rights movement, but we can look at events as tipping points.

The Revolutionary War had the Boston Massacre and Boston Tea Party, with meetings and responses that followed leading to the war. The Civil War can show how the expansion of the country into new territories created conflicts over the spread of slavery until the country was at war. *Brown v. BOE*, Rosa Park's arrest, and Dr. King's "I Have a Dream Speech" were key events leading up to the passage of the Civil Rights Act of 1964.

It's hard to pinpoint where we seem to be losing ground in race relations and even going backward. From a law enforcement perspective, the video of the Rodney King beating that played millions of times ushered in a new era. It is common now to take incidents on video and break them down with social commentary, helping people form opinions about what they are seeing. The narrative of the King tape easily could have been "don't run from the police or this is what happens." Instead it was if you are black and get stopped by the police, this is what happens.

An even bigger setback came less than five years later, also from Los Angeles. The arrest and trial of O.J. Simpson was a television spectacle. The defense team helped it evolve from a murder trial involving domestic violence to putting the LAPD on trial for what many believed was decades of mistreating African Americans.

Images of African Americans celebrating as a man was exonerated for the brutal murder of his wife had many white Americans shaking their heads in disbelief. Less than two years earlier Los Angeles jurors refused to convict two men for a vicious assault that occurred during the riots that followed the officer acquittals in the King beating. The two African American men had pulled a white construction worker, Reginald Denny, out of his truck during riots. Video clearly showed the men beat him severely including smashing a cinderblock on his head followed by a victorious dance around his unconscious body.

The jury may have felt they were discarding clear video evidence just as they perceived the jury in the King beating did. The message of this was payback was fair even though the victim was innocent. For those celebrating and others grieving the O.J. verdict, it was black versus white and black wins. It may for some have seemed like payback for generations of black versus white and white wins. Feelings of racial inequality existed long before these two cases, but mass media exposure helped the frustration of communities become those of a nation.

In 2015 President Obama made the statement "Communities of color aren't just making these problems up." He's well aware that a large portion of Americans believe just that. The comment was made following anti-police protests, indicating the problems he was referring to were racist cops. It can seem as though these experiences happen to every person of color in every community that is predominantly African American. These types of assumptions can label and put people into groups they don't see themselves belonging to or even want to be in.

If someone dares to break a stereotype, they can expect to be bullied or ridiculed. An African American student or adult who dresses conservatively, speaks articulately, and cares more about reading than sports may be accused of trying to act white. A white kid who listens to hip-hop, wears saggy pants, and uses slang may be told he is trying to act black. A coworker once confided in me that he was advised by another African American that he needed to find his "blackness." It's just as likely for a white person to be expected to associate with white coworkers and face criticism if they do not.

The school lunchrooms have always been examples of races voluntarily separating. Going back to the 1980s, lunch looked much like it does now. With a few exceptions, when given a choice, students divide and sit with their own race. Places of worship and social organizations also seem to voluntarily separate along racial lines.

It seems recently that things have been worse and the improvements that have been made are so fragile that a single act or comment can wipe out what seems like decades of progress. A person accused of racism can be left with the burden of proving they are not racist.

As kids grow up they are told, often by parents, which side of the racial line they should be on, and most just fall in place. African Americans may be told how white privilege still exists and that white people think they are superior. The idea of white privilege is that white skin will help you get a job, a promotion, college acceptance, and other opportunities.

America has rich and privileged white Americans, just as we have rich and privileged African Americans. Most of us are not in these categories. White Americans who live in poverty or paycheck to paycheck scoff at the idea of privilege. They instead may believe some African Americans complain too much and blame racism for daily problems that they also deal with. White Americans may perhaps see a double standard in having organizations, colleges, scholarships, networks, awards, or pretty much anything that is specifically for African Americans. Both races may fail to understand how the other could possibly be angry.

For every African American who believes white people have an unfair advantage there are white people who think all of the benefits go to black people. In the 1990s, the Richmond County (Georgia) school system welcomed their first African American superintendent. The next three superintendents were also African Americans, which led to grumbling that the African American members of the school board would not consider white applicants.

I can't know the motives of the school board, but I do feel sympathy for the new school superintendents, just as I would anyone who devotes themselves to succeed and have someone dismiss your achievement as an "I told you so" moment.

As true as it was that the last four superintendents were African American, it is also true that all of the previous superintendents were white. It is likely that African American candidates were not even considered for such a job thirty years ago. It's undeniable that in the history of America being African American has been more difficult than being white. Some may see this turnabout as fair play while others may see it as fighting past racism with modern racism.

None of us would want our hiring or promotions that were a result of our hard work disregarded because of our race. The idea of putting yourself in the shoes of another race is difficult, and most people have no desire to even try.

Hundreds of years ago if you were rich in America it meant you were white, but that did not mean if you were white you were rich. The rich white class did not distribute their wealth among their race in these days any more than they, or rich people of other races do today. I can attest that simply being born white does not come with a trust fund and a get-out-of-jail free card.

Among the middle and lower class there seems to be a lot of frustrated and angry white people for it to be such a privileged existence. Being white can be seen as having the challenges of everyone else plus the blame for the history of oppression in this country, not just against African Americans but also Native Americans, Latinos, and Asian Americans.

When I listed some of the jobs I've worked earlier, you may be surprised to know I have applied for a dozen other jobs that I was rejected for. I expected to make sergeant a dozen times at the sheriff's office and never did. I put in for and was interviewed to be the head coach of two different sports teams and was not offered the jobs. I know the feeling of picking out a car and furniture only to walk away with a credit rejection.

Each time I thought about what I may have done wrong or could have done better. I think one of the biggest disservices we can do to minority children is give them an "out" or an excuse for rejection, or even for their own shortcomings. We let too many kids believe that failure is not in their control and instead it is society keeping them down.

Many white Americans agree that institutional racism still exists with the intention of impeding African American progress, just as some African Americans believe other African Americans unjustly complain and blame white Americans for too many of their problems.

We must be willing to look at some of our practices and attitudes about racial reconciliation and realize that some of the things we are doing may be counterproductive.

The idea is not to have a winner or loser. Give up trying to convince anyone that race is the primary factor in regards to who struggles and who advances in today's society. We all feel as though we are struggling, we all feel like sometimes we are treated unfairly, and we all would like to blame someone else. In actuality, black and white Americans have more similarities than differences.

Another bad idea is talking more about race or at least how we talk about race. This country has a history of problems dealing with race, but the willingness to talk about it has never been a problem. The conversation cannot always be about how poorly African Americans are treated in this country. Even if that is what you believe, you should know that opinion is not universally accepted. That counterargument is that the difficulties of African Americans are no different than those of other Americans and we should not label someone as racist just because they believe we all have the same problems.

We frequently analyze and debate problems going back hundreds of years to behaviors that stemmed from colonization. Even if we go back 230 years when America declared its independence, or 150-plus years when the Civil War was raging, none these examinations will solve today's problems because many of our current problems have been created in the modern era.

White supremacists and black militants will never listen or change their hearts because they have no desire for unity. There are sadly some ideologies that may always exist; we just shouldn't promote them, and we should hope their support is minimal. For the rest of us, we have to continue moving past a divisive history that was in place before most of our ancestors arrived in this country.

While some believe that opportunities are disproportionate along racial lines, it's undeniable that African Americans live, work, and succeed across the country. If this country provides such great opportunities, why do so many people feel frustrated and hopeless?

The tragic deaths of Trayvon Martin and Michael Brown led to them becoming household names; the six to seven thousand black males killed each year by other African Americans are rarely a headline on the local news. Is it an accident that only the deaths of African Americans at the hands of white people or law enforcement get attention? Politicians, news outlets, celebrities, and criminals use these deaths to promote and profit from racial discord. It's not as nefarious as it may seem because most of the people promoting and profiting believe these deaths are in fact racially motivated. If you are a parent, I'm not sure if it's a consolation when you are burying a child to believe the death was politically motivated.

Following the 2008 election, even Americans who did not vote for President Obama knew this could be an opportunity to move beyond generations of strained race relations. The idea of unifying the country and looking beyond his own race may have been an unrealistic expectation and certainly not something his predecessors were expected to accomplish.

Some white Americans thought the election itself demonstrated that we had moved past race. Some African Americans looked to President Obama to improve a life they felt had been limited by the country's history of racism. One undeniable thing was that the election tapped into African American pride and united black America as never before. Even into his second term, children and adults of every socioeconomic class wore clothing and buttons celebrating the president.

I've been in homes, classrooms, and offices with portraits of the Obama family framed as though it was a portrait from their own family. I've met many of the president's supporters who could not tell you about his policies, programs, or beliefs and openly admit they did not care.

A fellow teacher proclaimed she did not want to hear any criticism of President Obama and she would support everything he did. This loyalty seemed blind but stemmed from the pride and the kinship for having the first African American president. The day following the election, my next-door neighbor pasted the front page of the newspaper on his garage door, where it remained for weeks. One thing is certain, the politics of racial division are beneficial.

I've worked security details when Rev. Sharpton was in Augusta for events honoring singer James Brown. Mr. Sharpton called out the youth in attendance on the image of wearing saggy pants, spoke against controversial rap lyrics, and emphasized the need for strong families and faith. These types of speeches are not the type of speeches that gain people notoriety or financial support. We are more likely to hear and associate Rev. Sharpton with divisiveness rather than as an advocate for personal responsibility.

One of the greatest things about President Obama is that he provides a positive image of an African American man that is not an athlete or entertainer. Regardless of politics, he is everything parents of any race would want their children to be. It is undeniable the president is highly educated, successful, and a devoted father and husband. As with others, the statements by the president that are divisive receive more attention both from critics and supporters.

The attention given to the remarks by the president and others on both political sides about police brutality and other issues can create anger that doesn't go away with an election. This anger manifests into not just words but action.

I'm still surprised at the times I've been called a racial slur. Usually it's a cracker, honky, or white devil. I've been told by students and suspects, "I don't like white people," "I hate white people," and "white people make me sick." One student told me he wished all white people would die.

One of the most disturbing statements I can remember was from a tenth grade student asking in all sincerity if white people could bring back slavery. This was around the time of Joe Biden's "They're going to put y'all back in chains" comment which was played repeatedly, perhaps out of context, for its shock value. The sad realization remains that many children are so overwhelmed with stories of hate, discrimination, and slavery that they feel personally connected to them.

Other comments that stumped me were things like "we ain't slaves" or "this ain't slavery time anymore." It seemed nonsensical to me for those things to be said in this the twenty-first century.

I can understand the current presence of frustration and vivid accounts of inequality going back even to the Jim Crow era. Many of the activists of that era, such as U.S. Representative John Lewis, who participated in the Freedom Rides, are still with us, and having experienced this firsthand may still feel resentment.

A question I can't answer is if there are African Americans in the twenty-first century who genuinely feel angry over slavery. A kneejerk response may be of course they do, but if so why? They never experienced it and no one alive or even a parent or a grandparent experienced slavery that last existed in 1865. If this anger does exist, where is it focused? Is it anger at all white people, Europeans, or Portuguese slave traders or just general anger with no face attached?

When encountering people who just seem angry, responding with anger just validates their feelings. I talked about my job interview with Dr. Mason at Laney High School, but I also had a second interview that took a peculiar turn. During the interview the principal of Glenn Hills High School, Dr. Wayne Frazier, asked what I thought a failing student looked like. I responded by saying I didn't believe there was a stereotypical "failing student."

Dr. Frazier rolled his eyes and then clarified by asking what race I thought was more likely to fail. I was shocked at his bluntness and irritated because it was clear he wanted or expected me to say black. Instead I explained I didn't think race was a determining factor on academic success. He abruptly cut the interview off, said thanks for coming, and started looking at papers on his desk.

Unexpectedly I was offered the job the next day but had already accepted the job at Laney.

Dr. Frazier's temperament reminded me of Joe Clark in the inspirational movie *Lean on Me*. Joe Clark tells students they are looked down on by society and considered trash. He does this in an effort to motivate students so they will succeed on a standardized test. If being told to pass the test because everyone hated them actually motivated those students, how much damage was done during the effort? These statements to impressionable students are almost impossible to reverse, and they will go through life feeling like people are out to get them.

Some people reject racism and the idea of race as outdated. In the early 1980s I remember being given a standardized form to fill out in middle school. A classmate sitting next to me got my attention and pointed to the section on the form marked "race." He smiled and marked "white" even though he clearly appeared black. More than thirty years later, I'm not sure if he was making a statement or a joke. Perhaps my classmate saw himself differently than what I saw. It is more difficult each day to pinpoint someone as a specific race, according to Pew Research, 19 million people in the 2010 U.S. Census identified their race as "other."

In 2014 Sweden, seeking to combat racism, eliminated the mention of race from all of its laws. Some have proposed doing away with the race boxes in America, and a CNN blog described those boxes as archaic.

Someone who was dedicated to eliminating racial identifiers was American Civil Rights Institute founder Ward Connerly. He has even proposed to make it illegal for data to be collected based on race, and advocated for Americans to refuse to declare their race. With America being so obsessed with race, it may seem impossible that we would ever take that type of action, but Connerly has been fighting this battle with his Racial Privacy Initiative for a decade.

The idea of black student unions and organizations can be viewed as divisive and confrontational. These organizations have at most times been very positive and encouraging, but they also pride themselves on activism. They are formed with the intent of promoting equality for African Americans and some have been around for more than a century.

At the University of Missouri in 2015, African American students who were protesting asked white students attempting to join the protests to leave. We've seen throngs of white students and adults joining protests in Ferguson, Baltimore, New York, and Chicago. These individuals are trying to demonstrate unity and support a cause they are not personally affected by.

In a washingtonpost.com article on November 24, 2015, by Yanan Wang, titled "More than 30 purported 'White Student Unions' pop up across the country," it lists a variety of social media pages and statements promoting ideas and new white organizations and even white student unions with phrases like "showing Whites... that it is okay to be White." I don't believe America wants or needs white students who feel left out starting these types of organizations, which would obviously be counterproductive in race relations.

Historically we've seen if a specific demographic begins to feel threatened, groups like these will emerge. Those who don't feel a kinship with the black student unions may see organizations that promote one race as unfair. One trademark of the millennials is they demand what they believe is fair play.

Over the last few decades we've seen protests not just about law enforcement, but from conservative groups such as the Tea Party to supporters of same-sex marriage. At times it can seem as though we are a nation of protesters. We even see crowds blocking streets celebrating sporting events.

There is a social aspect of being involved in a protest. On television while protesting some very serious issues, participants are often seen smiling and laughing. The pain and outrage of protesters in the streets and on college campuses is authentic, but that doesn't mean the causes of those feelings are always real. Our emotions can be manipulated by speeches, music, books, movies, or television programs. The reliability of what we see thanks to digital technology is even in question.

Experts can be as unreliable as video, as they are often on the payroll of different organizations and individuals. These experts are paid to make sure they only release information relevant and favorable to a certain point of view. Celebrities and athletes accumulate millions of fans and followers and shape the thoughts and beliefs of people who may otherwise have little or no opinion about certain issues.

Social media can help outrage spread across the country in an instant. One incident or allegation can spark a campus-or community-wide uproar. There seems to be a lack of consistency about what or who makes people angry.

Justice for Trayvon Martin and Michael Brown are popular themes of many protests still today. Many people do not accept that both cases were investigated, and in the Martin case an arrest and trial was conducted. In both cases physical altercations had occurred prior to the shooting, with Martin and Brown winning both of those.

The only things I know about George Zimmerman and Officer Wilson is what was provided by the media. It does seem as if they were NFL football players the outrage would be much less. Ray Lewis is a celebrated football hero with a nine-foot-tall statue in Baltimore despite being charged with brutally murdering two young African American men. Lewis was never acquitted and instead took a plea for his cover-up of the crime and resumed his NFL career.

Other NFL players have also been accused and convicted of murder, including New England Patriots Pro Bowl tight end Aaron Hernandez, who was convicted of murder. In 2012 Kansas City Chiefs player Jovan Belcher murdered his girlfriend before killing himself. Carolina Panthers player Rae Carruth is expected to be released soon after serving part of a prison sentence for arranging the murder of his pregnant girlfriend.

It would be too long of a list to describe NFL players' arrests and suspensions on cases including weapons, drugs, and domestic violence. Certain actions and behavior can trigger outrage in some cases but are dismissed in others. Radio personality Don Imus lost a brilliant, successful career for saying "nappy-headed ho" about female African American basketball players. Paula Dean lost a television show and endorsement deals when she admitted referring to an attacker using the "n" word in a private conversation with her husband.

NFL player Riley Cooper was recorded making threats against African Americans using the "n" word but remained employed and cheered as he scored touchdowns. Justin Bieber was recorded talking about killing African Americans, also using the "n" word, and talking about joining the KKK. Beiber's career barely hit a speed bump and he was even on a Celebrity Roast and praised by many African American celebrities including Kevin Hart and Snoop Dog.

There is not an acceptable level of violence, police brutality, or racism. If you are outraged and if it is authentic, then it should be consistent. If the "n" word is offensive, it should be offensive regardless of the context or race of the person saying it.

If you are concerned about the senseless killing of unarmed black men, it should be all killings regardless of the race or occupation of the person pulling the trigger. A mom may join in a protest if she is convinced race had something to do with her child's death, while the mother of a child killed by someone of the same race is equally devastated; they just get less attention.

At the beginning of this book I asked you to have an open mind and consider how many things that cause you anger and frustration are your own experiences and how many are other people's stories. Are you as concerned about what's going on in your own community as you are these big news stories? When you hear these stories, do you allow yourself to entertain the possibility that it could be exaggerated or that you may only be hearing one side?

Lastly, do you even want to get along? Do you want to have a positive relationship with law enforcement and between different races? When I stared teaching I took a saying from football coach Rick Neuheisel: "relentlessly positive." It is a standard I often fail to meet but always strive for. I try to use this when a student has a bad day, grade, or incident and always allow second, third, and forth chances. Even when having to discipline students, I remind them that tomorrow is a new day with new opportunities.

We can choose at any time to stop being angry, to stop blaming others for our hardships and to appreciate what we do have. We can at any time give others the forgiveness and understanding we would like to receive ourselves. All of this is contingent on our desire to move forward as a nation and unite as Americans with goals and dreams, and not in factions based on race or political parties.

It may seem like I'm dreaming of a world where we all hold hands while sitting under a rainbow singing "Kumbaya." I'm not. We are going to have so many legitimate differences on issues that are relevant in this millennium that we don't have to imagine that the problems and prejudices of decades and centuries ago still exists. What we are doing is not a continuation of racial strife we are creating it anew.

The reason people protest is the same reason they join gangs, the same reason they might join a cult, and the same reason they are susceptible to join terrorist groups. It's the need for people to feel like they are a part of something, like they are important. It's also the same reason they want to be professional athletes, actors, and singers and have a thousand likes of views.

People want their lives to mean something. It's why they fight against racism, sexism, and bigotry. It's the same reason they invent, create, and discover. Protesters want to leave their mark, but is it really about change or is it about the protest? Do people want to talk and resolve differences or is it just about jumping up, screaming, and pointing fingers?

A 2015 benefit entitled "Shining a Light—A Concert and Conversation About Race" opened with a montage of three black men killed during arrests and the Charleston Church murders. The police have been labeled by this show as the same as a racist mass murderer who killed innocent churchgoers.

This is the epitome of the problem, the narrative that every black person killed by someone who is not black is the product of racism, without acknowledging the far greater threat of African Americans being killed by gang violence at the hands of other African Americans. Making Americans angry is not difficult when you have a platform to disseminate information and opinions.

Reports and selective statistics outrage the American public and make them believe the narrative that the police and the country are out to get African American men. The numbers of black men killed by the police each year is in the hundreds. That number includes justified shootings when officers or citizens were also in danger, whether from an imminent threat or actually being shot and killed.

I have never met anyone who wished death, prison, poverty, or hardship on anyone because of their race or any other reason. Is it so unreasonable to believe we truly wish each other the best? Is it impossible to accept that every person knows we would be a better and stronger nation if everyone is successful, educated, and happy?

When asked, many protesters claim to be looking for justice, equality, and even freedom. This can leave many people in dismay that fellow Americans truly believe they don't have these things. If these rights don't exist, how would things be different if the changes were made? Do all of the changes involve being given something or reducing the number of white people?

One of the Ferguson arguments discussed earlier in this book was the need for more African American police officers, which means less white police officers. In the University of Missouri campus protests, they called for more African American teachers. We hear calls for more African American coaches, all of which means less white people.

Many schools and businesses actually have specific programs to recruit African Americans, and this has been going on for decades. They offer incentives ranging from preferential selection to monetary bonuses. Opportunities for success exist in this country for us all. These opportunities, however, are competitive as we all want to succeed, and whether you are a sports team, a business, or a school, they are all looking for the best. Hopefully no one believes they are entitled to something they did not personally earn.

When I was a growing up, my father and I played chess several times a week. Night after night I would take my loss, and each time my mother asked my father why he never let me win. My dad always responded that if I ever won I would know I had truly won and not because he had let me. Historically, African Americans have been denied the opportunity to compete for success. Those battles were fought and won, and for decades, as long as I can remember, race, gender, and even physical disabilities have not been barriers to success.

My wife and I had been dating for a while before someone asked me about dating an Asian girl. It took me a second to process. While she is obviously not white, it never factored into my decision to go out with her, and I had not taken it into consideration whatsoever.

I had never been out with another Asian girl and didn't have a "type." This was just a great person I met and we got along really well. Was it racist that I didn't take my wife's race into consideration while dating her? According to a segment on the "Shining a Light" benefit, it may have been. One of the hosts, John Legend, brought citizens of different races together to have a talk on race.

A white man who attended seem to offend an African American female by proclaiming that when he saw her he did not see her race; he just saw a person. It still has me perplexed: Are we even seeking a colorblind society? It always seemed like racism to see someone as a black man instead of just a man, but if he sees himself as a black man first and not as man, I'm not sure of the goal.

As a nation we are increasingly multi-racial and our families are blended. By forcing a black or white label on everyone, it also dictates how we should properly interact with one another. We are already doing it by saying white people need to be doing this and black people should be doing that.

It's not that we don't see each other's race, but the truth is most people don't care and hate it when people demand that they do. It needs to be accepted that we may have a number of categories that we fall under, but people who are busy with their own lives don't stop and think about other people's labels.

Not caring about your race doesn't mean I don't care about you. It just means that it is not a factor in my life and not a factor in how I feel about you.

A bunch of old, rich, white guys recognized in 1954 that this country should not be divided by race. They unanimously voted to overturn the "separate but equal" ruling from 1896 with the *Brown v. Board of Education* ruling.

We have moved rapidly toward integration and equality since that time, and I for one do not want to go back and I hope this country does not want to either. If we are forced to look at ourselves and separate ourselves based on race but also asking for equality, isn't that exactly what we are going back to? We have problems, but we are not as evil and racist as many of the protesters on the evening news believe.

Chapter 5

Violence and Hate in Entertainment

Gangs, parents, and the education system can have a profound impact on the type of citizens we are creating in this country. With all of their influence, the entertainment industry surpasses all of these and may be our kids' greatest teacher. The content is uncensored and easily accessible twenty-four hours a days, seven days a week.

A 2009 Nielson study showed 285 million Americans watch an average of 153 hours a month of television. If that's not enough, Americans consistently spend over $10 billion a year on movie ticket sales. Over 114 million fans tuned in to watch the Super Bowl in 2015. If television, movies, and sports don't provide enough entertainment, in 2013 *Grand Theft Auto V* made over $800 million in a single day.

All of this is only a fraction of the entertainment we take in. High school, college, and professional sports, concerts, and comedians are but a few of the spectator events we can attend. We stream and download everything from street fights to pornography. Entertainment not only influences opinions about what we love and hate, but it can give us ideas about what to do with that anger.

We all learn and gain images of behavior from the entertainment industry. I can remember listening to music to get pumped up before executing search warrants. One of the biggest investigations I worked was a dozen young men following the blueprint from the 1991 movie *New Jack City*. These men attempted to take over a housing project, establishing lookouts, manufacturing, and distribution points throughout the area. The ringleader even calling himself Nino Brown after the main character.

Just like these guys wanted to be drug dealers after watching this movie, I wanted to be a narcotics detective after watching *Miami Vice*. Police officers also get ideas from entertainment. Cops on TV cut corners to get the crooks, and the villains always get what's coming to them.

Go to the movies and watch the hero shoot the bad guy in the head. Spend forty dollars on pay-per-view to see mixed martial artists beat opponents until they are pulled off. Kill dozens, hundreds, even thousands of people in the virtual world of video games each week. Athletic accomplishments are celebrated by taunting and belittling fellow competitors. Bloody crime scenes and bodies are broadcast daily on the news. The main character of your favorite TV show is often a ruthless criminal. Pundits on news shows tell us twenty-four hours a day what we should be thinking and feeling.

Whatever your opinion on same-sex marriage or marijuana notwithstanding, there should be little debate that Hollywood has influenced perception on these issues and others. The entertainment industry has promoted a number of social issues in movies and television. The inclusion of gay characters as role models has contributed to increased tolerance and acceptance of homosexuality. Casual drug use is now seen as fun and harmless, and the outlook has shifted with several states moving to legalize marijuana.

One thing that Hollywood doesn't take credit or blame for is how they promote hate, violence, and criminal activity. Popular shows like *CSI* and *Law & Order* can serve as a blueprint for criminals. They teach how to clean a crime scene or resist interrogation tactics, which can help criminals avoid detection and conviction.

Torture and sexual assaults can be seen on basic cable at all hours of the day. The cinematic gore often exceeds what a real crime scene looks like. Most of us can appreciate that these shows are meant for entertainment; however, it's not unusual to see crimes and crime scenes inspired by popular shows and storylines.

The idea of copycat crimes is not unique, but the exposure due to the growth of TV provides even more graphic content to more viewers. According to research there were 10,000 televisions in American homes in 1945. The reports shows that the number of televisions grew to 219 million by 1997 up to 285 million in 2007.

Any effort to influence what is being shown is vigorously shouted down as censorship. The entertainment industry through all its mediums has desensitized us to violence. We look forward to watching main characters committing horrendous acts or the bad guy meeting a brutal demise.

Breaking Bad featured a former teacher making and selling methamphetamines. The series *Dexter* not only portrays the main character as a serial killer but also as a crooked cop taking the law into his own hands.

In years of working as a narcotics detective, numerous dealers admitted being inspired by movies such as *Scarface*. They never cared about the brutal endings of such movies, but instead saw how being a coldblooded drug dealer was the road to riches.

Our opinions about guns are also influenced by the entertainment industry. Liberals blame guns for violence;

conservatives point at violence to reinforce the need for guns. The idea that guns are a way to send messages or solve problems is reinforced not only on television but in video games that our children grow up playing.

Video games simulate violence with realistic scenarios in the same manner that technology is used to train law enforcement and the military. I can remember when the Columbine High School shooters' fascination with the game *Doom* was publicized. If this was a problem in 1999, today's video games are dramatically more realistic and violent.

Today we rarely hear about the gaming or television habits of random shooters, not because they don't have them but the idea that gun violence may be related to anything but the availability of guns is not politically expedient.

While games do have rating systems that outline content, they are far from a deterrent. Indulgent parents continue to buy these games, often unaware of what's in the games, and send kids to their room for hours of uninterrupted and unmonitored gameplay. Most of us are not going to be influenced by games, but some individuals due to mental illnesses such as schizophrenia cannot differentiate between the imaginary and the real world.

The influence of the entertainment industry on racism is just as powerful as its effect on violence. I can vividly remember Eddie Murphy on a popular *Saturday Night Live* skit talking about hating white people. He said, "Their hair is wavy, their lips are thin. But worse than white women, I hate white men." This skit was hilarious but also so popular that Murphy had to step out of character to address a fan letter from a kid who also hated white people. Murphy tried to explain that he did not actually hate white people and it was a joke. Like most successful jokes, it was based on some truth and resonated with a lot of viewers.

Popular comedian Chris Rock, during a televised comedy routine, chastised Jessie Jackson for his anti-Semitic views. He spoke as though he were talking directly to Rev. Jackson and explained that black people should not hate Jews. He paused, and in a loud voice proclaimed that black people should hate white people. It may seem as though I'm not recognizing a joke, but I did laugh the first time I saw it and have been a Chris Rock fan going back to his *SNL* days and television show *Everybody Hates Chris*. What is troubling is that you'll notice after watching the routine a few times that the camera pans to the audience; the joke does not incite as much laughter as it does applause.

It is so accepted to proclaim hate against white people that it hardly raises an eyebrow. Kanye West tells fans if a clerk asks if she can help them, it's actually racial profiling because they think black people are there to steal.

Oprah Winfrey even claims she experienced racism when a clerk in another country hesitated to let her hold a $38,000 purse. Due to a large public following, celebrity comments about racism can have an even greater impact. It can become a "here we go again" moment, a confirmation of how difficult it is for minorities to live in America. It can also result in other Americans also saying "here we go again," with more people complaining and blaming others for hardships we all experience.

Tiger Woods probably handled racism better than any celebrity I can recall. He has been one of the most successful golfers in history and easily the most successful African American golfer ever. Tiger had so many opportunities to exploit racism in a sport that is played at historic clubs like Augusta National, which hosts The Masters and did not have a black member until 1990.

Even when racism was directed toward him, Tiger Woods refused to be drawn in. An example was when fellow golfing champion Fuzzy Zoeller made a "fried chicken" comment with racial overtones. Woods quickly dismissed it and let Zoeller off the hook. Compare that to Samuel Jackson, who was mistaken by a KTLA interviewer for being the spokesman on a credit card commercial that was actually Laurence Fishburne. Jackson berated the apologetic reporter for the entire interview, refusing to accept the apology or even discuss the movie he was on to promote. It's impossible to know how serious Jackson was, but people looking for "I told you so" moments would believe he was completely serious.

Many of our celebrities earned their fame from movies and shows that highlight racism and violence, so we should not be surprised when they echo some of the sentiments of the characters they portray. The concern is not trying to change the celebrities; they are so out of touch with the people they are paid to entertain, why bother. The concern is instead the influence they have on fans as we empower them beyond what they do on the screen or stage.

While movies and video games impact how young adults and children see the world, they also give dangerous solutions on how to react to our problems. If the messages don't come through in entertainment, then—in what begrudgingly still calls itself the news—pundits from every conceivable point of view have a forum to present themselves as an authority on a variety of subjects.

In the 1990s, Rush Limbaugh's television show offered a nightly dose of how immoral and corrupt President

Clinton was. I had heard of Limbaugh's radio program but never listened to talk radio. Rush was intelligent and his arguments were well thought out. I found him easy to agree with, and his opinions became many of my own. I have to admit after a while it became exhausting. It was mentally tiring each day being angry and feeling like Clinton was ruining the country, and every show provided new information and scandals.

Years later it would be the same thing, except instead of analysts fueling anger toward Clinton it was targeted at George W. Bush. News channels became a forum not just for attacking Bush but for partisan commentators to go after almost everyone and everything. Instead of just being mad at the politicians, we became angry at entire political parties, businesses, and schools as analysts called us to action.

For every person's critic, you can find one of their supporters. Into the Obama administration, social media has made every issue a Twitter or Facebook post, giving the unqualified and uneducated an opportunity to spread opinions to the masses.

The result of this influx of information and often misinformation is more division and anger. Every opinion, no matter how radical or irrational, can find an expert and allies to support what may be an absurd thought. Even people who aren't angry or upset can watch a few minutes of television, listen to talk radio, or just browse the Internet and become frustrated or find support for their argument or opinion.

Dr. Lamont Hill is a brilliant, accomplished professor and has been a commentator for years on various cable shows. His calm, confident demeanor makes everything he says sound like an absolute, not an opinion. I became a fan of Dr. Hill when he was an opposing opinion to Bill O'Reilly, and I would often note that he made his points better than Mr. O'Reilly even though I did not always agree with him.

I love watching and listening to Dr. Hill, but it seems when it comes to race relations, Dr. Hill is far from a uniting voice. His words are more likely to incite a protest than a peace march. Each time an incident involving African Americans makes the news, you can look for Dr.

Hill to find a racial angle. Dr. Hill has made comments like "young black lives don't matter in America," and "it's open season on black men." If it's open season, the logical inference from Dr. Hill is that the hunters are white people, law enforcement, or both. The inflammatory nature of his remarks will be ingrained into parents and children, who will repeat them as fact.

A kid who thinks his life doesn't matter and the life of other black males doesn't matter will not cherish either. Children will not process Dr. Hill's words with any opposing views or even in the context of what may have sparked the discussion. They'll just take them for what they are—a warning that people are out to get you.

The Trayvon Martin case is an example. Dr. Hill and others could not take the incident and hold the person who committed the act responsible. They had to make it a larger indictment of America.

When racism is thrown on an incident, it can muddy waters that should be clear. From the details that were made public about the Trayvon Martin killing, I felt like the shooter George Zimmerman could have been charged differently and convicted if the motive of racism had not been so emphasized and, if instead, his actions were put on trial.

As a deputy sheriff, I worked dozens of assault and homicide cases. While my experience as an investigator was in narcotics, I worked and trained with violent crime investigators and prosecutors. In the Zimmerman case, I would have thought the prosecution would pursue primarily a stalking charge, which I believe most people agreed happened. It also seems like Martin did beat up Zimmerman, but if the incident only occurred because Zimmerman was breaking the law by stalking, a conviction would have been more likely. Instead it came down to whether Zimmerman followed and killed Martin because he was black, and that was much harder to prove than just laying it out. The facts could have shown that Zimmerman stalked Martin even after being told by a dispatcher not to. That crime then led to a confrontation that led to a death. A manslaughter charge with the stalking conviction could have resulted in a lengthy prison sentence.

When race is made the issue, people on both sides circle the wagons. The fatal result of putting race at the forefront of disputes is that we are taking generations of kids who should be proud and thankful to be Americans and making them hate the country in which they live.

We can see this lack of appreciation and even contempt for their country with students at American colleges who proudly stomp on the American flag—a country that is probably giving the same students grants and loans so they can even attend. We seem to be at a point that we are unable to disagree and still respect one another.

It's okay to think President Bush or President Obama did things that were harmful to the country. What's illogical to think is that either of these men, or past presidents for that matter, wanted to harm our country. Every president regardless of their political affiliation wanted to have a successful presidency and wanted the country to be safe and great; to think otherwise is foolish. President Herbert Hoover wanted to end poverty, not cause the Great Depression. G. W. Bush wanted to be the education president, not the war president. The healthy way to approach this is to acknowledge that our political leaders act out of a belief that what they are doing is a good idea, and it is okay to disagree without disrespecting.

Cable news programs on both conservative and liberal networks will incorporate both sides of an issue followed by the host explaining what you should think about that night's topic. Civility on television does not get high ratings, and the news has become a reality TV show that is scripted for dramatic effect. The risky part of this is that there is not a screening process for who watches these shows.

If Rush Limbaugh makes a point, he has no control over how an unstable individual will react. Likewise, if Rev. Al Sharpton voices an opinion, people may not take that call for action as getting out and voting. When we allow people to chant things like "no justice, no peace," that is clearly a call for violence and is occasionally acted on.

Whether it's talk shows, television, movies, or video games, the entertainment industry, as much as they want to deny it, has a responsibility for the content they distribute to the public. The celebrities, athletes, and commentators who have loyal fan bases should realize their comments and posts have repercussions. If what they have to say is not positive or productive, they should think twice and realize how supporters can construe their comments and cause harm.

It's not just the content of the entertainment but the amount. History describes "Bread and Circuses." It's when Rome was falling while citizens cheered and celebrated the spectacle of gladiators fighting in arenas.

Today, instead of gladiators it's NASCAR and football. Instead of bread its chicken wings and hamburgers. This is not only a thing with sports; your local theater can show twenty different movies with multimillion-dollar budgets. You can buy a barrel of popcorn and a forty-four-ounce soda while you are whisked away to a make-believe world for two or three hours. If that's not enough, simply flip on one of hundreds of television channels. If you don't like what's on TV, you can always stream thousands of hours of shows and movies online.

In case we forget how important the entertainment industry is, they remind us on a regular basis with award shows. All of our entertainment is intertwined with corporate affiliations that have investments in multiple ventures. The same companies that give us the news also make movies and TV programs. They also own sports teams and contribute to political campaigns. These corporations that comprise the entertainment industry are so invested in everything, it would be financially counterproductive to attempt to regulate or reduce the amount of entertainment.

It is up to the public to speak with our votes and wallets. As much as we say it, none of us wants absolute freedom, which would mean we have no laws or regulations. We need government censorship and control on the content allowed in video games, movies, and television. As standard entertainment has become about promoting anger, violence, drug use, and racism, we must figure out when responsibility outweighs content described as freedom of speech.

Earlier I referenced how Hollywood was able to change American attitudes about same-sex marriage and marijuana. I don't think consumers were writing the studios asking for this content to be included in more programming. Instead networks responded to pressure from organizations such as Gay & Lesbian Alliance Against Defamation (GLAAD) to change their programming. The CEO and president of GLAAD, Sarah Kate Ellis, said in an interview following the Supreme Court's ruling on same-sex marriage that their Network Responsibility Index had helped reshape the television landscape by pushing television networks to include inspiring LGBT characters and storylines that moved acceptance forward. Ms. Ellis stated the move now is toward transgender, and we already see these programming changes.

My point is not about same-sex marriage but instead about how our opinions and beliefs can be intentionally and successfully changed with a concentrated effort from the entertainment industry. If by including gay characters on television it can influence millions of Americans to accept same-sex marriage it stands to reason that attitudes leading to the acceptance of violence have been influenced for decades through TV shows, movies, and video games

Chapter 6

The Millennials:
Disconnected and Discontent

Many young adults and college students involved in protests and demonstrations are considered millennials. When you think of the millennials, you can't help but think of technology. Unfortunately, the generation is so connected to that technology that they are disconnected to some of our most valuable personal skills. "Please" and "thank you" are not some of our more popular text messages that are sent. In the '90s, my own kids had to be told to put their phones away during dinner and to stop wearing headphones around the house.

The millennials were raised by parents who grew up using their own cell phones and computers. Children today are lucky if they can get their parents to stop texting or to take out their earbuds to have a conversation. The closest thing to family time may be when everyone is in the car together. At home everyone has their own device, whether it's a computer, tablet, cellphone, TV, or more likely all of the above.

When a kid thinks of making a parent proud, they realize Mom and Dad's attention is dominated by celebrities and athletes. If a child thinks about what their mom and dad are interested in, they may realize it's on TV or the Internet.

Reality TV has shown this generation that talent and intelligence are no longer a requirement for becoming a celebrity. If your morality doesn't stand in the way, posting risqué selfies can be a popular way to get attention. What drives millennials is not as much education and accomplishment as it is the desire for likes and views from posts and comments.

In the movie *Dumb and Dumber To*, one of the characters has a flashback of putting peanut butter on his private parts and having his dog lick it off. In the county I live in, a man was arrested for trying to make a viral video that he could post by reenacting the scene with his young child and dog.

These types of staged incidents are not rare, and people will sacrifice almost anything or anyone for what is perceived as fame. Kids have always done anything they could to get attention, but with the advances in technology, acting out is now available for millions to see. Anyone who has access to the Web can watch and there is no taking anything back, so technological indiscretions live on forever. Every day, criminal trials occur where things that were looked up on the Internet and text messages that were sent years ago are retrieved and used.

Technology also influences millennials and the relationships they build. I am still amazed when people who live in the same house post messages on Facebook to one other. I would not be surprised if people sit in the same room texting each other.

Another thing millennials do is have fake fun. When I go out it's easy to see people with phones and cameras taking selfies and videos to post on social media. The big smiles, hugs, and fun often disappear when the camera and video are turned off.

Millennials have a unique approach to relationships. A guy trying to convince a girl to have sex is nothing new and also vital to the continuation of the human race. The counterculture of the 1960s called it "free love" when they wanted casual sex. For the millennials it's not just about convincing girls to have sex or anything bordering on love; what many men want now is for women to belittle and humiliate themselves. They expect this not only in bed but in videos and pictures that can easily be posted, saved, and shared.

Sexual relationships today are less about intimacy but instead about behavior that could be seen in hardcore pornography. The entertainment industry pushes this on our children and young adults as normal behavior, while virginity, monogamy, and abstinence are ridiculed.

It's not uncommon for women attempting to be modern and hip to call themselves bitches and even refer to other women in this way. It should be no surprise that many women behave less than ladylike when characterizing themselves in these derogatory terms.

It is absolutely no different than when an African American refers to themselves and other African Americans using the "n" word. These terms are the most disrespectful way possible to refer to women and African Americans, and yet many in these two groups accept these terms and surrender their dignity.

Both are likely to demonstrate behavior and attitudes that fit these insulting terms. Imagine how a woman would behave who says yeah I'm a "b," or an African American who would say yeah I'm an "n." People who want and demand to be respected must not engage in or tolerate these disparaging categorizations.

It's true every older generation thinks the next is doomed to fail. While I have criticism for the millennials, it's meant to be more warnings and advice than doubting their potential. A lot of people today are not content with the idea of finding a job, settling down, and raising a family.

When I hear the term "single mother," I think of a widow or a divorcee with a deadbeat dad not paying child support. I think of a mom putting her own dreams on hold while working multiple jobs raising her children. While this is true of some single moms, I also think about the *Maury Show*. On the *Maury Show* young women routinely appear with multiple men undergoing DNA tests trying to find the father of their baby appearing on a large screen behind them. It plays out on afternoon TV with tears and cheers as men hope to be cleared from eighteen years of child support following encounters with women they are not even in relationships with.

Millennial parents have several nontraditional trends when having and raising children. In 2008 the U.S. Census showed that more than 40 percent of all children in the U.S. were born outside of marriage. A 2014 washingtonpost.com article by Cheryl Wezstein unmarried cohabitating parents were described as "fragile families" because they often break up after a few years. If this alone is not a concern, another study from the American Community Survey found single-parent families were six times more likely to live below the poverty line. Moreover, poverty has a clear correlation to incarceration rates as well as children from low-income families being less likely to graduate high school or attend college.

Out-of-wedlock birthrates are even higher for African Americans: over 70 percent. We see a de-emphasis on the importance of families among all millennials, and the reason the statistics are even higher in the African American community is that it is increasingly culturally acceptable.

A 2011 msnbc.com report by Linda Carroll, titled "1 in 5 US moms have kids with multiple dads," reports 59 percent of African American mothers compared to 22 percent of white mothers have children with multiple fathers. I can't say how often this is carless birth control, but I have known students who openly talk about wanting to have children not later in life but right then.

An example of ideas being cultural is demonstrated in a popular rap song from The Notorious B.I.G. called "Big Poppa." It's actually a catchy song featured in several movies including *Hardball* about inner-city kids playing baseball. A recurring line is that he sees "some ladies tonight that should be havin' my baby." The song also drops the "f" bomb, says the "n" word, and talks about his gang, alcohol, and drugs—all pretty standard content for hit rap songs.

There is no shortage of music today with positive, uplifting messages; the Pharrell Williams song "Happy" has to come to mind. The music of the millennials has a strong influence on their perception of what is appropriate, and it's not just rap and hip-hop sending these messages. Negative influences in music cross all genres. Popular country groups including award-winning Florida Georgia Line also promote casual sex and drug use to millions of young, impressionable listeners. Rock has a long history of promoting bad behavior, and the group Hinder had their most popular song in 2005: "Get Stoned."

Millennials also see the world in a different way than previous generations. While finishing my master's degree in 2009, already in my forties, I was usually the oldest in all of my classes. In the multicultural education class, I found myself one of the few who felt America was the greatest country on Earth. The idea of a global world is very millennial, and I was the only one who resisted the idea. To me a global world seemed unpatriotic and counter to the idea of American excellence.

In a Pew Research article by Katie Riley titled "A Generational Gap in American Patriotism," the majority of all generations in the survey, including millennials, believed freedom is the reason for America's success. Millennials, however, saw a 15 percent drop from other generations when it came to whether America is still the greatest country, and many do not consider themselves patriotic. The decline in patriotism in millennials is a concern, and it is even more dramatic among African Americans.

In a 2010 bet.com article titled "Are Blacks Less Patriotic Post-9/11?" Britt Middleton cites several Pew

Research studies showing a 10 percent drop from 2002 to 2010 among African Americans who considered themselves extremely patriotic. In asking if they were proud to be an American, only 36 percent characterized themselves as extremely proud.

Patriotism has a direct link to military service. Joining the military in any capacity requires patriotism, but people of all races join the armed forces for many reasons including money for education and job skills.

Army Special Forces, Air Force Special Operations, and Navy SEALs are some of the most difficult and dangerous jobs in the world. These jobs are also listed among the highest needed categories in the armed forces. Due to the extreme physical requirements, even when applicants are found for these positions few are able to complete the training.

African Americans comprise only 5 percent of the Army's Green Berets and only 2 percent of the Navy SEALs and Air Force Special Operations. Compare that to 68 percent of NFL players being African American and

76 percent of NBA players. It shows African American males statistically work very hard to become elite athletes but have little desire for elite military service. Everyone has different reasons for pursuing individual careers, but being a professional athlete and a member of the military have several things in common including fitness, loyalty, and sacrifice.

An athlete willingly sacrifices his body for his team and wants to win just as a service member in combat does. Commentators will even describe athletic contests as battles and wars, a description I'm sure most veterans would not agree with.

The two large discrepancies between the careers are pay and praise. Few military members will ever earn even $100,000 a year compared to the millions a year professional athletes can make. Almost every student I have taught in both middle and high school expects to be rich, and many hope to make it as a professional athlete.

The percentage of African Americans in the military has seen a decline among millennials. A 2014 *USA Today* article titled "Military Backslides on Ethnic Diversity" by Greg Zoroyoa cited Pentagon numbers showing a 10 percent drop in African American soldiers and Marines over the last twenty years. It also showed that African American students during that period interested in joining the military has decreased by 15 percent.

There are plenty of millennials and African Americans who are proud of this country, but there should be little doubt that those numbers are declining. Even when you can fill positions, millennials present another problem. Military.com states that a difficulty in training millennials is their need for constant recognition. This fits the mentality of wanting likes and views for posts and getting trophies and awards for simply participating.

As a teacher I see kids starving for attention and willing to do almost anything to get it. Parents' lives no longer revolve solely around their children. Single and married parents often both work full-time and sometimes multiple jobs. Single parents often maintain active dating and social lives. It's not unusual for parents to take vacations without the kids, and even in a traditional nuclear family it is common for children to leave school and go straight to some type of practice or afterschool activity.

In other ways the millennials are the best generation yet. The advantages over previous generations with technology enables them to learn at an incredible pace. They can collaborate with great minds around the world and research millions of sources in seconds. The negative is that many of the millennials see success as all or nothing.

Some of the millennials I went to college with passed up jobs and worked part-time and continued living with their parents into their twenties until the exact jobs they wanted opened up. Millennial athletes have the same mentality of getting precisely what they want. They will practice and work out for hours each day, leaving little or no time for schoolwork.

In the event that a millennial doesn't get into the right job or get that scholarship, they are likely to do nothing and consider their effort a failure rather than settle for something else. They may also blame their failure on anything and everything but themselves. It's a hard lesson to learn as an adult that we don't always get the trophy and award even if we think we deserve it.

For decades I've used a quote with my own kids and kids I've taught and coached: "Never confuse potential with accomplishment." People who are capable of doing great things may not possess the work ethic or have the patience to achieve that success. We hear "life is a marathon, not a sprint," but for this generation it's a series of sprints and the idea of working the same job for twenty or thirty years may be gone.

The other thing that millennials may refuse to accept is that not everyone has the potential for everything. We expect schools to send every kid to college. Students who don't meet the standards can enroll in college by taking remedial classes and eventually get degrees in fields that don't even have a career path.

For $50,000 a year, a student can attend Columbia University and major in a number of general studies programs in almost anything you can think of. Columbia even shared on their webpage in January 2014 a story defending degrees in humanities titled "The 'Useless' College Majors of the World's Most Successful People."

For many millennials, college is a transition point between high school and figuring out what career they want. It's a transition that comes with massive debt and regrettable behavior fueled by binge drinking and drug use, both of which are seen as a part of the "college experience."

As a teacher, I love learning but I do not believe students should go to college and take out loans to take courses that do not lead to a degree without a career goal. Learning can be done at the library or on the Web and does not require a degree to verify something was learned. Going to college just to say you're in college is one of the dumbest things smart people do.

While I've tried to generalize some behavior and habits of millennials, if they are nothing else they are unpredictable. Some of the students I've taught fit every stereotype you can think of: tattoos, long hair, love to wear hoodies, saggy pants, and gold grills covering their teeth. They were also some of the most intelligent and courteous people I have ever met.

The other thing about today's generation of kids and young adults is that they care. They care about animals and the environment. They care about inclusion. They go out of their way to make sure races, ethnicities, religions, gender, and sexual orientation is respected. It's not saying they can't be mean and opinionated, but they are educated and aware.

Politically, the excitement about President Obama and his potential to change the political landscape in America may not be carrying over. The new fad of millennials is to reject labels, and the Republicans and Democrats are all about them.

The millennials provide hope when it comes to racism and so much more. My last advice to them would be that while it's popular to be against society, it's easier to make changes from the inside. If you want to make changes in the police department, become a police officer. If you want to make changes in education, become a teacher.

The same goes for politics, religion, and business. It's a corny old line, but if you want change, be that change.

Chapter 7

The Politics of a Divided Nation

Our first commander-in-chief warned the new nation of what could be our most destructive division. Despite his warnings, factionalism tears at the very fabric of our society. Factions affect every area of our lives, and efforts to oppose them can cost you anything from employment to your life.

George Washington passed up the opportunity to be king after rallying the nation to victory in the Revolutionary War and encouraging acceptance of the then controversial U.S. Constitution. For all of his diplomatic skills, he acknowledged being unable to negotiate a compromise between the rival political parties. In his Farewell Address in 1796, Washington explained: "The alternate domination of one faction over another, sharpened by the spirit of revenge, natural to party dissension, which in different ages and countries has perpetrated the most horrid enormities, is itself a frightful despotism."

Political parties play voters like puppets pitting one against the other for votes and control. The parties themselves are controlled by financial contributors, activists, lobbyists, and interest groups that help shape party and candidate platforms. If a candidate rejects any part of the platform, it can mean the loss of money and support. Nobody knows this better than Colin Powell, who would have likely been the 2000 Republican nominee instead of George W. Bush, and could have been the first black president.

Colin Powell's leadership during the Gulf War made him extremely popular, and Republicans were excited at the possibility of him as a candidate. Powell, however, broke with the Republican platform by saying he would support gun control and abortion rights and would not support mandatory school prayer. These statements quickly eliminated Powell as a prospective candidate.

Conservative interest groups could not get past these issues. Powell, who was obviously a conservative, served in the Bush administration and became the first African American secretary of state. He supported the Iraq War and defended Bush against allegations that relief efforts following Hurricane Katrina had anything to do with race. This man could have been a great conservative president on so many issues but never got the chance because our political parties do not compromise.

Just as Powell was disqualified because of his centrist beliefs, a Democratic candidate not supporting abortion rights or gun control would not find a very warm welcome within their party. To ensure loyalty, candidates may even be asked to take pledges on certain issues. It is sad that individuals who may be able to build bridges and move this country forward are excluded by their willingness to work with the other party.

Republicans and Democrats create loyalty in voters by instilling fear. Voters don't just disagree; parties spend so much time bashing the opposition that loyal Democrats and Republicans actually hate each other.

Republicans make their supporters believe that the Democrats want to raise taxes to take their money to pay for abortions and give money to able-bodied Americans who refuse to work. Republican voters are made to believe that Democrats want to take their guns and Bibles and give their jobs to immigrants.

Democrats have convinced supporters that Republicans are racist, intolerant homophobes who want to deprive poor children of healthcare and starve them by cutting off food stamps. Democratic voters are made to believe that Republicans and their support of gun rights are responsible for all of the murders in this country and that Republicans, given the opportunity, would take away African Americans' right to vote and try to put more of them in jail.

The political parties work very hard to keep this strife going because it means votes, and for politicians there is nothing more important. Republicans do not want to reach an agreement with Democrats on gun control. As long as gun owners believe that by electing a Democrat they will be left unarmed with criminals running free, they will vote Republican.

Democrats want Republicans to be perceived as racist. If they can convince the majority of the African American voters that by electing a Republican the black community will suffer, they can count on that voting bloc.

The anger runs so deep that constituents do not even want their elected officials interacting with the other party. In a 2015 *USA Today* article by Luke Kerr-Dineen, then Speaker of the House John Boehner discussed the backlash after developing a friendship and playing golf with President Obama. "If I go down to see President Obama, the right begins to wonder what I'm up to. The left begins to wonder what the President is up to."

The politicians think these are switches they can flip on and off around elections. They sometimes forget that their words sink in, and when it comes time to get things done it's tough to convince supporters you should be working with someone you spent millions of dollars convincing them was evil.

Politicians are reluctant to criticize constituents or reconcile with political foes, especially those from opposing political parties, for several reasons. It is imperative to political success to build coalitions of loyal supporters, and if they were to attempt to rein in the radicals and their rhetoric, that support could turn against them. Fanatics are also willing to put their money where their mouth is, and if they believe a candidate or party supports their issue they will contribute and raise money.

Politicians' values evolve as public opinion shifts. Republicans who railed for years against the Affordable Healthcare Act gave the presidential nomination to Mitt Romney, who had implemented an almost identical plan in Massachusetts when he was governor. President Obama is quick to point out how the history of racism continues to hinder African American progress and equality, yet considered a fellow Democrat and Ku Klux Klan recruiter, the late Senator Robert Byrd, a friend.

Republicans have fought against same-sex marriage for decades, but VP Dick Cheney, who supported same-sex marriage, remained very popular among conservatives. First Lady Barbara Bush openly supported abortion rights but remained immune to criticism from Republicans. Democrats would never emphasize Republicans who share some of their core beliefs because that would not help elect Democrats.

Voters are told to take these issues into consideration and vote straight Democrat or straight Republican. Voters are warned that if they want to stop or support certain issues, they need to help a specific party gain control of the House and Senate.

Going into the primary season, candidates urge voters to support party nominees even after they have spent millions of dollars telling voters a fellow Republican or

Democrat is not qualified. Voters are asked to vote along party lines even before they know who the candidates will be.

Years ago Republicans said they needed a Republican in the White House. It does not even enter into the thought process that the future unknown Republican candidate could be worse than the future unknown Democratic candidate. Democrats are exactly the same; they want to control the White House regardless of the matchup.

Undecided voters are ridiculed, and some states are so consistently red or blue that candidate's do not even bother to campaign, already predicting the outcome without even having a candidate in place. In the 2012 presidential election undecided voters were estimated at 6 to 12 percent. Instead of wondering why some voters are undecided months and years before elections, we should ask why we all aren't.

Our votes and support should not be automatic, and a single issue should not allow us to reject a candidate who may serve us honorably. The candidates and parties would hate the idea of having to fight for each of our votes, and that may just be the chance we have to change politics in America.

Conclusion

We live in dangerous times but also a time of great opportunity. One thing I tell my students when preparing for an exam is how important it is to "know what you don't know." If we think we know everything, we are prepared to learn nothing.

If African Americans feel discriminated against in the criminal justice system, education, and other areas, it's important to figure out why so many people feel that way. If we don't agree, an alternative to why statistical discrepancies exist must be given.

I hope in this book I've provided some insight into why I believe it is unrealistic that law enforcement officers target minorities. I've tried to also present some ideas on how law enforcement can improve, and I acknowledge there may be bad officers but I do not believe the system is bad.

When it comes to millennials we have to realize we're not going back to the good old days, and for this generation they may look back on this time as their good old days. We have to reject things like gangs and hate speech and find commonality in knowing that we live in a blessed nation that immigrants are still willing to risk their lives each day trying to come to. We must keep entertainment, politics, and sports in perspective and realize that, yes, we only live once but that should be a life of purpose, and that our greatness will not be measured by what we do for ourselves but, instead, what we do for others.

Bibliography

Agiesta, Jennifer. "Race and Reality in America: Five key findings." CNN.com. November 25, 2015. http://www.cnn.com/2015/11/24/us/race-reality-key-findings/index.html.

American Civil Rights Institute. *About Mr. Ward Connerly.* http://acri.org/about-ward-connerly/.

Carroll, Linda. "1 in 5 U.S. Moms have Kids with Multiple Dads, Study Says." NBCNEWS. com. April 1, 2011. http://www.nbcnews.com/id/42364656/ns/health-childrens_health/t/us-moms-have-kids-multiple-dads-study-says/#. VnbAoDbSnIU.

Chaudhary, Neil., Nichols, James., Tsoni, Julie., and Williams, Allan. "Determining the Relationship of Primary Seat Belt Laws to Minority Ticketing."

U.S. Department of Transportation Office of Behavioral Safety Research. September 2011. www.nhtsa.gov/staticfiles/nti/pdf/811535.pdf.

Cillizza, Chris. "Who are the "undecided" voters? And what the heck are they waiting for?" The Washington Post. October 9, 2012. https://www.washingtonpost.com/news/the-fix/wp/2012/10/09/who-are-the-undecided-voters-and-what-are-the-heck-are-they-waiting-for/.

Coates, Ta-Nehisi. "Understanding Out-of-Wedlock Births in Black America." The Atlantic. June 21, 2013. http://www.theatlantic.com/sexes/archive/2013/06/understanding-out-of-wedlock-births-in-black-america/277084/.

COLLEGEdata. College Profile Columbia University, 2015. http://www.collegedata.com/cs/data/college/college_pg03_tmpl.jhtml?schoolId=399.

Columbia College Student Advising, The 'Useless' College Majors of the World's *Most Successful People*. January 29, 2014. https://www.cc-seas.columbia.edu/csa/blog/useless-college-majors-worlds-most-successful-people#.VnbeCDbSnIU.

Duffy, Nick. "Mission accomplished? GLAAD discontinues report on TV's LGBT characters." Pink News, September 3, 2015. http:// www.pinknews.co.uk/2015/09/03/mission-accomplished-glaad-discontinues-report-on-tvs-lgbt-characters/.

FBI Reports and Publications. *2011 National Gang Threat Assessment – Emerging Trends.* https://www. fbi.gov/stats-services/publications/2011-national-gang-threat-assessment/.

FBI Reports and Publications. *2013 National Gang Report.* https://www.fbi.gov/stats-services/publications/national-gang-report-2013.

Georgia Department of Education. *Georgia Performance Standards – Social Studies.* https:// www.georgiastandards.org/standards/Georgia%20 Performance%20Standards/United-States-History.pdf.

Graser, Marc. "Grand Theft Auto V Earns $800 Million in a Day, More than Worldwide Haul of Man of Steel." Variety, September 18, 2013. http://variety.com/2013/digital/news/grand-theft-

auto-v-earns-800-million-in-a-day-more-than-
worldwide-haul-of-man-of-steel-1200616706/.

Hilton, Judith. "Race and Ethnicity in Fatal Motor
Vehicle Traffic Crashes 1999 – 2004," NHTSA's
National Center for Statistics and Analysis,
May 2006. http://www-nrd.nhtsa.dot.gov/
Pubs/809956.PDF.

Kerr-Dineen, Luke. "John Boehner says fellow
congressmen won't let him play golf with
Obama". USA Today Sports. July 30, 2015.
http://ftw.usatoday.com/2015/07/john-boehner-
says-fellow-congressmen-wont-let-him-play-golf-
with-obama.

Melia, Michael. "Navy Seeks to Adapt Training for
Millennials." Military.com. September 29, 2014.
http://www.military.com/daily-news/2014/09/29/
navy-seeks-to-adapt-training-for-millennials.html.

Middleton, Britt. "Are Blacks Less Patriotic Post-
9/11?" BET.com. September 8, 2011. http://
www.bet.com/news/national/2011/09/09/are-
blacks-less-patriotic-post-9-11-.html.

National Law Enforcement Officers Memorial Fund, *Law Enforcement Facts*. http://www.nleomf.org/facts/enforcement/.

Newport, Frank. "Gallup Review: Black and White Attitudes Toward Police," Gallup, August 20, 2014. http://www.gallup.com/poll/175088/gallup-review-black-white-attitudes-toward-police.aspx.

Nielsen. "Americans Watching More TV than Ever; Web and Mobile Video Up Too." May 20, 2009. http://www.nielsen.com/us/en/insights/news/2009/americans-watching-more-tv-than-ever.html.

Pallotta, Frank. "Super Bowl XLIX posts the largest audience in TV history." CNN Money. February 2, 2015. http://money.cnn.com/2015/02/02/media/super-bowl-ratings/index.html.

Phillips, Noelle. "Survey: Denver police officers say they treat minorities fairly." The Denver Post, June 19, 2015. http://www.denverpost.com/news/ci_28347306/survey-denver-police-officers-say-they-treat-minorities.

Pro.boxoffice.com. December 2015. http://pro.
boxoffice.com/statistics/yearly.

Ravitz, Jessica. "Out-of-wedlock births hit record
high." CNN.com, April 8, 2009. http://www.
cnn.com/2009/LIVING/wayoflife/04/08/out.
of.wedlock.births/index.html.

Reilly, Katie. "A generational gap in American
patriotism." Pew Research Center. July 3,
2013. http://www.pewresearch.org/fact-
tank/2013/07/03/a-generational-gap-in-
american-patriotism/.

Roberts, Sam. "New Census Numbers Show
Recession's Effect on Families." The New York
Times. August 27, 2013. http://www.nytimes.
com/2013/08/28/us/new-census-numbers-show-
recessions-effect-on-families.html?_r=0.

Rundquist, Solveig. "Race to be scrapped from
Swedish legislation." The Local. July 31, 2014.
http://www.thelocal.se/20140731/race-to-be-
scrapped-from-swedish-legislation.

Sagalyn, Daniel. "Report: U.S. Military Leadership
Lacks Diversity at Top." PBS Newshour. March

11, 2011. http://www.pbs.org/newshour/
rundown/military-report/.

Simpson, Ian. "Baltimore homicides top 300 for
year, worst since 1999." reuters.com. November
14, 2015. http://www.reuters.com/article/us-usa-
crime-baltimore-idUSKCN0T400H20151115.

Starr, Alexandra. "How the legacy of Amadou Diallo
lives on in New York's immigrant community."
Public Radio International (PRI). February 05,
2014. http://www.pri.org/stories/2014-02-05/
how-legacy-amadou-diallo-lives-new-yorks-
immigrant-community.

Vanden Brook, Tom. "Pentagon's Elite Forces Lack
Diversity." Marine Corps Times. August 6,
2015. http://www.marinecorpstimes.com/story/
news/nation/2015/08/05/diversity-seals-green-
berets/31122851/.

Wang, Yanan. "More than 30 purported 'White
Student Unions' pop up across the country." The
Washington Post. November 24, 2015. https://
www.washingtonpost.com/news/morning-mix/
wp/2015/11/24/more-than-30-questionably-

real-white-students-unions-pop-up-across-the-country/.

Wezstein, Cheryl. "Census: More first-time mothers give birth out of wedlock." The Washington Times. July 8, 2014. http://www.washingtontimes.com/news/2014/jul/8/census-more-first-time-mothers-give-birth-out-wedl/?page=all.

Zoroya, Gregg. "Military Backslides on Ethnic Diversity." USA Today. February 17, 2014. http://www.usatoday.com/story/news/nation/2014/02/17/black-history-month-military-diversity/5564363/.

Acknowledgements

Writing can be a solitude endeavor with many hours, days, weeks, and months writing and rewriting. It's a struggle trying to remember those thoughts that seem to come up at time and place impossible to write them down.

Through the years my wife Mia, children Wes, Liana, Shane, and Derik have patiently listened to my ideas providing feedback and motivation.

I have encountered so many people in my life, both personally and professionally that have taught me tolerance and acceptance. Some of the negative people

I've come across have influenced me as much as the positive people in my life.

Taking ideas and turning them into a book was more of a challenge than I expected and finding an accomplished writer and editor willing to see the vision for this book was a blessing. David Aretha gave me guidance well beyond what I could have asked from an editor and encouraged me to keep the book focused. Finally he put me in touch with Rob Price and Gatekeeper Press who took the edited manuscript and turned it into a book that I hope will be used a positive tool for change and an awakening of what the real problems are and what they are not.